*Social Relations
in Byron's Eastern
Tales*

Social Relations in Byron's Eastern Tales

Daniel P. Watkins

Rutherford • Madison • Teaneck
Fairleigh Dickinson University Press
London and Toronto: Associated University Presses

Associated University Presses
440 Forsgate Drive
Cranbury, NJ 08512

Associated University Presses
25 Sicilian Avenue
London WC1A 2QH, England

Associated University Presses
2133 Royal Windsor Drive
Unit 1
Mississauga, Ontario
Canada L5J 1K5

The paper used in this publication meets the
requirements of the American National Standard for
Permanence of Paper for Printed Library Materials Z39.48-1984.

Library of Congress Cataloging-in-Publication Data

Watkins, Daniel P., 1952–
    Social relations in Byron's Eastern tales.

    Bibliography: p.
    Includes index.
    1. Byron, George Gordon Byron, Baron, 1788–1824.
Eastern tales.   2. Byron, George Gordon Byron, Baron,
1788–1824—Political and social views.   3. Social
contract in literature.   4. Politics in literature.
5. Social problems in literature.   6. East in
literature.   7. Near East in literature.   I. Title.
PR4372.E278   1987   821'.7   85-46014
ISBN 0-8386-3287-4 (alk. paper)

Printed in the United States of America

For Joanna Foster

Contents

Acknowledgments

I am grateful to all those who have discussed the ideas in this book with me over the past four years. I am especially indebted to Gayle S. Smith, who directed my dissertation on Byron, and to Steve Badrich, David Sebberson, and Terry Hoagwood, who challenged me to sharpen my thinking about Romanticism, who read portions of the book in manuscript, and who encouraged me as I worked to formulate my critical perspective. I also owe a special debt of gratitude to Jerome J. McGann, who offered much helpful advice and encouragement at a time when they were particularly needed, and to John A. Thompson, who many years ago introduced me to the serious study of literature. My greatest debt is to Joanna Foster, without whose spirited conversation and intelligent criticisms this project would have been impossible.

In addition, I wish to thank The Johns Hopkins University Press for allowing me to reprint here (in somewhat revised form) chapter two, which first appeared in the pages of *ELH*, and the editors of *Studies in English Literature* for allowing me to withdraw chapter five, which had been accepted for publication in their journal. Finally, I am grateful to several presses for kindly granting me permission to quote from their copyrighted materials: Oxford University Press, for permission to quote from *Lord Byron: Complete Poetical Works*, vol. 3, ed. Jerome J. McGann; *Coleridge: Poetical Works*, ed. Ernest Hartley Coleridge; and *The Prelude; or, Growth of a Poet's Mind*, ed. Ernest de Selincourt; and Harvard University Press, for permission to quote from *Byron's Letters and Journals*, ed. Leslie A. Marchand.

Note on the Texts

Quotations from Byron's Eastern Tales are taken from *Lord Byron: The Complete Poetical Works*, vol. 3, ed. Jerome J. McGann (Oxford: The Clarendon Press, 1981). References to McGann's commentaries appear in the text as *BCPW*. Quotations from all other poems by Byron are taken from *The Works of Lord Byron: Poetry*, 7 vols., ed. Ernest Hartley Coleridge (1898–1904; reprint, New York: Octagon Books, Inc., 1966). References to Coleridge's commentaries appear in the text as *Poetry*. Quotations from Byron's Parliamentary speeches are taken from *The Works of Lord Byron: Letters and Journals*, vol. 2, ed. Rowland E. Prothero (1898–1901; reprint, New York: Octagon Books, Inc., 1966), and are cited in the text as *LJ*. Quotations from Byron's letters and journals are taken from *Byron's Letters and Journals*, 12 vols., ed. Leslie A. Marchand (Cambridge: The Belknap Press of Harvard University Press, 1973–82), and are cited in the text as *BLJ*.

*Social Relations
in Byron's Eastern
Tales*

1

Toward a Context for Studying Byron's Eastern Tales

URING his five years in England between 1811 and 1816, Byron did not, in
his opinion, write good poetry. Of the shorter pieces he produced during
this period, he believed his sonnets "To Genevra" to be "the most puling,
petrifying, stupidly platonic compositions" (*BLJ* 3:240), while "The Devil's
Drive," an experimental work modeled on Coleridge and Southey's "The Devil's
Thoughts,"[1] was "wild, rambling, unfinished" (*BLJ* 3:240). His longer and
extremely popular Eastern Tales were viewed with equal distaste. While he
occasionally showed pleasure in learning that they were finding an enthusiastic
audience, he generally thought they were inferior works. *The Giaour* was "foolish
fragments" (*BLJ* 3:105), *The Bride of Abydos* was "horrible enough" (*BLJ* 3:160),
and *Lara* was "too little narrative—and too metaphysical" (*BLJ* 4:295). Further,
they were hurriedly written, *The Bride* having been composed in four days and
The Corsair in ten days, which Byron took to be proof of "my own want of
judgment in publishing" (*BLJ* 4:77). If the tales were popular, he said, it was not
because they were of superior quality, but, quite the reverse, because of poor
public taste (see for instance *BLJ* 4:77). That he was not simply erecting a
Byronic defense against possible criticisms is clear from remarks made in later
years. In 1820, while asserting confidently that such works as *Werner* and *Heaven
and Earth* (now commonly deemed inferior poetry)[2] eventually would "be pre-
ferred to any I have before written" (*BLJ* 9:92–93), he remained firm in his
conviction that the poetry from his Years of Fame was worthless, likely "to
interest the women" (*BLJ* 9:125) and little more.

But if these poems fell below Byron's own standards of poetic excellence, they
nevertheless remain central to the Byron canon. The tales are particularly
important, for, despite their avowedly escapist content, they engage at every turn
the conditions under which they were created and thus stand as surprisingly
comprehensive symbolic formulations of the world as Byron saw it. They are, in
other words, vivid examples of what Jerome McGann calls "dramas of displacement," poems in which "actual human issues . . . are resituated in a variety of

15

idealized localities."[3] Even if they are not self-consciously intellectual or socially concerned, they are intellectually compelling, both as embodiments of Byron's world and as highly imaginative critiques of the disturbing abuses and injustices at the center of this world.[4]

The most important feature of the tales in this regard is their projection of the complex network of relations that defines and ultimately controls social reality. Specifically, the tales describe the pervasive cultural attitudes, practices, and beliefs which, under certain circumstances, not only limit human independence, but in fact support reactionary and morally destitute social systems. Further, they locate these political and ideological concerns within a comprehensive, if crude, conceptual framework that helps to demystify them, and thus to undermine their seemingly absolute control over social life. As Byron put it, acknowledging almost with embarrassment the serious dimension of the poetry written during his Regency years, "In rhyme, I can keep more away from facts; but the thought always runs through . . . yes, yes, through" (BLJ 3:209).

The social interest of the tales is obscured not only by their subject matter, but more importantly by Byron's thinking during these years, which is often very inconsistent, confused, and hidden behind a Byronic exterior of combined nonchalance and whimsicality that deflects serious inquiry. It is not surprising, for instance, to find him vacillating between enthusiastic ventures into social and political life on the one hand, and, on the other, feelings that his time in England was being "frittered away" (BLJ 4:22), or in the same breath voicing his strong support for Napoleon and a Republic, while also claiming that "The more I see of men, the less I like them" (BLJ 3:243). But such contradictory statements should not be taken to mean that Byron was incapable of serious social thought. As he himself understood, he lived in confusing times, "times of paradoxical servility" (BLJ 4:62), which threatened all clear thinking and deep conviction. The important point is not that particular statements contradict other statements, but rather that Byron inveterately analyzed and imaginatively wrote about social questions, and that he most often placed considerations of human experience within an encompassing social context. Despite certain outward inconsistencies, he held by a fairly coherent and fundamental social principle, which is expressed concisely in a letter to William Harness written in late 1811: "The circumstance you mention at ye. close of your letter is another proof in favour of my opinion of mankind, such you will always find them, selfish & distrustful, I except none.—The cause of this is the state of Society, in the World every one is to steer for himself, it is useless, perhaps selfish to expect any thing from his neighbour; but I do not think we are born of this disposition, for you find friendship as a school boy, & Love enough before twenty" (BLJ 2:150).[5] This important statement provides the necessary starting point for studying Byron's thought during these years. While perhaps on one level it recalls the sentimentality, say, of Wordsworth's "shades of the prison house" lament, at the same time it reveals how strongly Byron felt the pressure of social circumstance, and, moreover, it focuses the powerful (if submerged) social imagination controlling much of his poetry. Further, it goes a long way toward explaining his frequent shifts from withdrawal to commitment, from hope to despair, because it emphasizes that ongoing, inescapable, and at present corrupt social life resists all consistency and denies all claims of individual autonomy, thus implying that real solutions to human problems must be public rather than private. This perspective implicitly rejects popular assumptions about "natural" or private man as too limited and reductive—as too dependent on pure subjectivity—and attributes human characteristics to specific social and historical situations.

This is not to suggest that Byron is exempt from the subjectivist and idealist tendencies that are defining characteristics of Romanticism, and that recent historical reassessments of Romanticism have stressed. Catherine Belsey remarks: "One of the main thrusts of Romanticism is the rejection of an alien world of industrial capitalism, recurrently signified in images of death, disease and decay. Poetry claims to create a living world, fostered by nature but springing essentially from the subjectivity of the poet, from what Coleridge calls the Imagination, a mode of perception which endows the phenomenal world with a vitality and an intensity issuing ultimately from the soul itself. . . . The Romantic vision, though it needs the phenomenal world for its realization, transcends and transforms the material and the mortal."[6] McGann, towards the conclusion of *The Romantic Ideology,* notes the futility of this Romantic position, with specific reference to Byron: "In the end Byron's poetry discovers what all Romantic poems repeatedly discover: that there is no place of refuge, not in desire, not in the mind, not in imagination. Man is in love and loves what vanishes, and this includes—finally, tragically—even his necessary angels."[7]

But if Byron shares these ideological limitations with his contemporaries, at the same time his response to transcendental desires and possibilities is usually less speculative and contemplative than theirs, and this gives his social perspective a different emphasis. Refusing to cast his poetic vision in theological, philosophical, or "natural" terms (as Blake, Shelley, and Wordsworth do), Byron instead imagines whole societies (some exotic, others admittedly melodramatic) wherein power relations and systems of thought stand exposed. This focus enables him to dramatize human values and practices wholly as constituent elements within an encompassing *social system,* without relying on transhistorical or subjectivist principles to explain them. While his Byronic heroes exhibit powerful wills and egos (so much so, in fact, that other matters often seem merely backdrop) and exude mystery and stubborn independence, their values and conduct are always shown to arise from specific controlling networks of social relations.[8]

Byron's letters and journals display his intense interest in questions of system and thus provide an important basis for assessing his social thought. In the 1813–14 journal, for instance, he speaks regularly and easily of politics and society in terms of their systematic qualities. Describing Napoleon's defeat and banishment to Elba in April 1814, he remarks: ". . . and here we are, retrograd-ing to the dull, stupid old system,—balance of Europe—poising straws upon king's noses, instead of wringing them off" (*BLJ* 3:218). At another point in the journal, and in a slightly different tone, he considers the international scope of his poetry, and speculates playfully upon its ability to overthrow the binding system of modern thought: "I like the Americans, because *I* happened to be in *Asia*, while the English Bards and Scotch Reviewers were redde in *America*. If I could have had a speech against the *Slave Trade, in Africa*, and an Epitaph on a Dog, in *Europe* (i.e., in the Morning Post), my *vertex sublimis* would certainly have displaced stars enough to overthrow the Newtonian system" (*BLJ* 3:236). This same emphasis is evident in his letters. Expressing once to Lady Melbourne his frustrations with British government and society, he threatened to leave the country again and to return only if "there is a prospect of alteration in the whole system" (*BLJ* 3:69). Even his responses to criticism of his poetry often were slanted towards questions of system, though, to be sure, he seemed to ridicule the idea that his verse in any way could be systematic. In a letter to Annabella Millbanke, he explained that the "Anti-Byron," a long critical poem sent to Murray for publication, was intended "to prove that I am the *systematic* reviver of the dogmata of Epicurus—& that I have formed a promising plan for the overthrow of these realms their laws & religion by dint of certain rhymes" (*BLJ* 4:82).

Such examples as these, along with many others (see, for instance, *BLJ* 4:332), suggest that if Byron was not entirely systematic in his thinking, he was at least aware of and responsive to concepts of system, especially with respect to topics of a social and political nature. Moreover, he understood that every system is predicated upon a knowable set of assumptions and that systematic analysis must stand or fall according to the viability of these assumptions. It is precisely on these grounds that he dismissed the critic attacking his ostensible Epi-cureanism: ". . . he [the critic] assumes at first setting out my *Atheism* as an incontrovertible basis & reasons wisely upon it—the real fact is I am none—but it would be cruel to deprive one who has taken so much pains of so agreeable a supposition" (*BLJ* 4:82).

Byron's intellectual development drew heavily upon an active and powerful tradition of social thought which, with growing authority, determined the issues of serious inquiry during his day. It is evident that he knew very well not only the popular ideas of such contemporary political thinkers as Burke and Fox,[9] but more importantly the line of thought including Hobbes, Locke, Rousseau, Hume and others who helped to develop, or who challenged, the social-contract theory, the most widely discussed and influential theory of society at this time. Yet he never simply and faithfully adopted the perspectives of these thinkers; while he accepted many of the categories they used in studying society, he questioned and departed from certain fundamental positions, particularly the assumption that individuals and society can in any way and on any level be separated.

Although during this period Byron never mentions by title any treatises on social contract, he makes frequent references to its proponents and detractors, especially Locke, Rousseau, and Hume, and his jottings in one of his Cambridge notebooks show that he had long known their works.[10] He seems to have been particularly influenced by Locke's and Rousseau's classification of society in terms of family, law, religion, the state and so on, and by their careful study of the social dimensions of war, slavery, liberty, and individualism. The Eastern Tales, in fact, appear at times to be methodical analyses of these respective concerns, giving the impression that Byron was consciously examining and extending social-contract categories in schoolbook fashion.

Of greater significance, however, is the point of contention between Byron and the social-contract theorists. Locke and Rousseau adopted an individualistic premise in discussing society. Their writings trace what they considered to be man's original private hardships to show how these were lessened by a social compact. Locke states as one example: "To avoid [the] State of War . . . is one great *reason of mens putting themselves into Society.* . . . For where there is an Authority, a Power on Earth, from which relief can be had by *appeal,* there the continuance of the State of War is excluded, and the Controversie is decided by that Power."[11] Or, as Rousseau puts it, "the human race would perish if it did not change its way of life"; only by "form[ing], by aggregation, a sum of forces that can prevail over the resistance" can humanity survive.[12]

This position is predicated upon the determining assumption that man first was *not* social and that then he *was* social, that there was initially "a state of Nature" in which man possessed "natural freedom," and then a state of society in which man enjoyed "conventional freedom."[13] An additional assumption which should not be overlooked here and which, in his letter to Harness (quoted above), Byron clearly rejects, is the Hobbesian notion that individual man, in his original state of nature, was basically selfish and destructive and had to be brought under the control of some larger authority which could contain and direct these dangerous traits. Social agreement worked very well, according to the theory, because, while its limiting context weakened man by checking many of his most basic impulses, it also prevented his needless injury and destruction, and even provided him with a workable framework for extending his laudable creative and self-preserving powers: ". . . since there is no associate over whom one does not acquire the same right one grants him over oneself, one gains the exact equivalent of everything one loses, and more force to preserve what one has."[14]

Byron's poetry demonstrates that the social-contract scheme not only fails to explain continued suffering and injustice, but in fact helps to perpetuate human atrocity by following a self-negating path of thought, that is, by taking an *assumption* as an intransigent norm. The underlying and unquestioned acceptance of an absolute dichotomy between individual and society, between natural destructiveness and social preservation, locates man's "real" character in a domain which is isolated from moral and social essence and which is in effect *self*-interested, *self*-defined, *self*-consuming. Further, such an assumption assigns controlling power to an external authority—i.e., because man's fundamental selfishness prevents him from productively managing his own affairs, he must submit to a larger, more "benign," managing system.[15] All of the tales reflect these concerns by presenting social situations overcome by their own inherent misunderstandings. This is the intellectual and imaginative strength of the tales: they provide a systematic critique of conventional notions about society and erect a shaky but visible alternative to individualistic perspectives of society. Even if they are not confident in their assessments (as they certainly are not), and even if they do not establish a fully workable position, they offer a rough sketch of new possibilities in social imagination and analysis.[16]

Byron's unwillingness to accept on faith traditional intellectual principles such as those underpinning social-contract theory did not result simply from his abstract analysis of certain logical inconsistencies in the work of important thinkers, but developed in large measure from his studied attempt to address (or to avoid, as was sometimes the case) various material circumstances of the day. The shaping influence of events surrounding him has been argued convincingly by David Erdman, who has traced in detail Byron's movements and political connections during this period, demonstrating his efforts to construct a viable, independent, and serious political position in a complex public climate (see note 4, above). It is not necessary here to retrace this ground, but we might build upon it by sketching briefly some additional general matters which certainly would have had a significant bearing on Byron's thinking as well as on his aesthetic choices at this time.

While they never figure directly in the tales, the Napoleonic Wars assuredly fired Byron's imagination, as they constitute the largest, most immediate, and most sweeping event of the age, bringing before the public mind not only the sheer power and complex strategies that characterized modern warfare, but also an encompassing set of ideas about the exciting possibilities—and dangers—of restructuring society entirely. At least initially, most of the Romantic writers saw the Wars as a struggle for liberty, and thus their support for Napoleon ran strong. (Indeed, most European intellectuals, even those from countries fighting against Napoleon, viewed the Wars in this manner.) Napoleon's presence, marked by military genius, charisma, and courageous resistance to tyranny, introduced a new ethical consideration into popular thought, best suggested perhaps by Shelley's remark that "no man has a right to be respected for any other possessions, but those of virtue and talents."[17] Only when the liberation aspect of the Wars began to diminish, and Napoleon abandoned his original principles in favor of imperial conquest, did such English writers as Wordsworth, Coleridge, and Southey (to name only the most famous) withdraw their support of the French general and adopt conservative, sometimes reactionary, political views. As Coleridge despairingly described France after Napoleon invaded Switzerland in 1798:

> O France, that mockest Heaven, adulterous, blind,
> And patriot only in pernicious toils!
> Are these thy boasts, Champion of human kind?
> To mix with Kings in the low lust of sway,
> Yell in the hunt, and share the murderous prey;
> To insult the shrine of Liberty with spoils
> From freemen torn; to tempt and to betray?
>
> ("France: An Ode," 78–84)[18]

Wordsworth's sentiments were virtually identical, as his early hopes for France were utterly dashed by the crowning of Napoleon as emperor:

> . . . to close
> And seal up all the gains of France, a Pope
> Is summoned in to crown an Emperor—
> This last opprobrium, when we see a people,
> That once looked up in faith, as if to Heaven
> For manna, take a lesson from the dog
> Returning to his vomit; when the sun
> That rose in splendour, was alive, and moved
> In exultation with a living pomp
> Of clouds—his glory's natural retinue—
> Hath dropped all functions by the gods bestowed,
> And, turned into a gewgaw, a machine,
> Sets like an Opera phantom.
>
> (The Prelude, 11. 358–70)[19]

The confusion and despair which arose as the Wars unfolded reflect the personal intensity with which writers watched international events, and their desperate hope to see liberty achieved at last. Within the larger context of historical development, however, this view of the Wars as an initial fight for liberty which gradually turned into a pursuit for personal power is incomplete. In a very real sense, the Wars were a specific, vivid, mirror-image of what was happening to European culture in general and constitute not so much a reversal as a progression. For the liberation being ushered in was on one level simply a new form of exploitation. This is suggested by the fact that Napoleon's continued success depended increasingly on the plunder of the very states he had liberated, or which were already republics (for instance, Switzerland). The frightening consequence was a powerful contradiction that eventually destroyed Napoleon's military campaign, but that nevertheless continued apace in the deeper structures of daily life after the Wars, thus serving as one of the formidable legacies of this period. This crucial point clarifies substantially the pervasive social impact of the Napoleon years and, moreover, helps to explain why many contemporary and later social thinkers (for instance, Cobbett and Ruskin) frequently grounded their analyses of society upon regressive idealizations of the past.[20]

One end toward which the Wars were irrevocably moving was a new society and a new conception of society. It is now a commonplace that, in the words of one historian, the Wars cracked "the structure of the old social order and laid the foundations of the modern bourgeois state,"[21] helping to create the economic, political, and ideological systems which subsequently prevailed. This development is seen most readily in England, which, though an opposition power, was motivated by the same bourgeois impulses as France.[22] In England, economic growth escalated dramatically during the Wars, as trade and industry (thanks at least in part to Pitt's war finance policies) found ways to combine patriotism and profit. As Cobbett wrote in 1802, "A race of merchants and manufacturers and bankers and loan jobbers and contractors"[23] came to the forefront of British finance because of the Wars, replacing the economic control traditionally exercised by old-line nobility. One effect of this growth of capital as a definitive political weapon was, at least for a short period, to make nobility and labor (whose real wages were being reduced substantially by the Wars) brothers in resistance, though to little real avail. (For evidence of this we need look no further than to Byron's attitude towards his Rochdale holdings, or to his frame-breakers speech.) It is the bourgeois ethic embodied in this economic triumph that came to prevail among revolutionaries and opposition alike. In this larger view, the transmogrification of Napoleon's fight against tyranny into a war for imperialism was simply one sign of the consistent and determined historical process that wove the concept of liberty inextricably into an exploitative social fabric.[24] A. L. Morton's description of Britain's position after the Wars is precise: "The British bourgeoisie came out of the war ready to consolidate a world monopoly for the produce of their factories and to begin a period of hitherto unimagined advance."[25] England was free, and its claim to dominate nations was legitimate.

A more positive consequence of the Wars to which Byron would have been particularly sensitive was the new realization that revolutionary change on a large scale was possible and that not only political institutions but also ideas and feelings could participate in this change. Of this consequence, E. J. Hobsbawm states that "it was now known that revolution in a single country could be a European phenomenon, that its doctrines could spread across the frontiers. . . . It was now known that social revolution was possible, that nations existed as something independent of states, peoples as something independent of their rulers, and even that the poor existed as something independent of the ruling classes."[26] Wordsworth's famous lines from *The Prelude* express this new consciousness very well:

> Now was it that *both* found, the meek and lofty
> Did both find, helpers to their hearts' desire,
> And stuff at hand, plastic as they could wish,—

Were called upon to exercise their skill,
Not in Utopia,—subterranean fields,—
Or some secreted island, Heaven knows where!
But in the very world, which is the world
Of all of us,—the place where, in the end,
We find our happiness, or not at all!

(ll. 136–44)

The belief that people in fact could determine the course of history inspired a new intellectual interest in society. There arose, as John Kinnaird puts it, "a theoretic commitment to a vision of society, or of political reality," which endured throughout the period: "Napoleon's regime was often seen and judged, even by lukewarm on-lookers, as perhaps the only 'enlightened' alternative to the hoary anachronisms that opposed his power." Even if particular atrocities were attributable to Napoleon, he nevertheless was "advancing the cause of modern civilization and the rule of cosmopolitan law against the darkest strongholds of superstition and despotic 'barbarism'" by (in Hunt's words) "cultivat[ing] . . . the human intellect."[27]

Byron's attempts to come to terms with the European situation—and particularly with Napoleon—are well known both from his many comments in his letters and from references in his poetry, and I do not wish to do more here than touch glancingly upon the subject in an effort to suggest ways the events of the war years informed his thought. Napoleon's abdication in 1814 strongly affected Byron, forcing him to reassess his expectation that France ultimately would prevail and create a republican Europe. If he was half joking when he remarked to Moore that Napoleon's fall "would draw molten brass from the eyes of Zatanai" (*BLJ* 4:93), he later wrote quite seriously and openly to Annabella Millbanke that "Buonaparte has fallen—I regret it—& the restoration of the despicable Bourbons—the triumph of tameness over talent—and the utter wreck of a mind which I thought superior even to Fortune—it has utterly confounded and baffled me" (*BLJ* 4:101). When Napoleon escaped from Elba a year later, Byron was elated: "I can forgive the rogue for utterly falsifying every line of mine Ode [to Napoleon Buonaparte]. . . . And now, if he don't drub the allies, there is 'no purchase in money.' If he can take France by himself, the devil's in't if he don't repulse the invaders, when backed by those celebrated sworders. . . . It is impossible not to be dazzled and overwhelmed by his character and career. Nothing ever so disappointed me so much as his abdication" (*BLJ* 4:284–85). Although hero worship admittedly inspires these remarks, much more underlies their enthusiasm. As Jerome McGann reminds us, Byron had made "an intense personal investment" (*BCPW* 3:457) in Napoleon. The French general was for Byron, as he was for many, the very embodiment of revolutionary process; Napoleon's fate was synonymous with the fate of revolution, and (more importantly) a sign of the credibility of revolutionary thought. Napoleon was talent, his enemies tameness; Napoleon was liberty, his enemies *invaders*. If he failed, then the terms of Byron's social analysis (and his social hope) were invalidated, rendered pointless against the powerful "reality" of status quo culture. That Byron's complicated view of Napoleon was intricately connected to his broader social analysis is stated clearly in his response to Waterloo: "Every hope of a republic is over, and we must go on under the old *system* [italics mine]. But I am sick at heart of politics and slaughters; and the luck which Providence is pleased to lavish on Lord [Castlereagh] is only a proof of the little value the gods set upon prosperity" (*BLJ* 4:302). Napoleon's every move, his various triumphs over and defeats at the hands of status quo culture, constitued new developments in radical social change, obligating Byron perpetually to examine and to reexamine entirely his own views on politics and society, especially his understanding of revolutionary process. His ongoing critiques of Napoleon from diverse perspectives mark one effort in this appraisal.

Several short poems written between 1814 and 1816 elaborate the difficulties and hopes which Byron attached to Napoleon. The bitterness he felt upon learning that Napoleon had abdicated is suggested by the epigraph to the "Ode to Napoleon Buonaparte," taken from Gibbon's *Decline and Fall,* which stresses the "shameful[ness]" of admitting defeat in one's efforts to better humanity, even when capitulation preserves one's life "a few years." The ode itself is more probing, examining the nature and possible accomplishments of a revolutionary politics. At the center of the poem is both a pained expression of the hope and virtue Napoleon had held forth to mankind, and at the same time a studied criticism of why, precisely, he destroyed the very inspiration he had ignited. Napoleon's defeat, for Byron, crystallized a very sensitive and complex point about social participation and leadership, namely that individual strength alone is dangerous and ultimately inadequate:

> By gazing on thyself grown blind,
> Thou taught'st the rest to see.
> With might unquestion'd,—power to save,—
> Thine only gift hath been the grave,
> To those that worshipp'd thee;
> Nor till thy fall could mortals guess
> Ambition's less than littleness.

(12–18)

Here is the central difficulty, the irreducible paradox to which Byron returned repeatedly in verse, seeking to understand it in order to lay it to rest, and it focuses upon the ideas—conceptual frameworks—governing human activity. The "lesson" (19) of historical events to which the poem is most responsive is that Napoleon misunderstood the nature of public and private life. His public good was underpinned by his private ambition; as his victories and accomplishments increased, his pursuit of power intensified, until his ego isolated him entirely from the context of his deeds—in a sense, public life, by the sheer greatness it offered, aroused and then paralyzed the private life. This essential conflict could be put to rest only when one pole was made to serve the other, and of course this is ultimately what happened, destroying Napoleon: "triumph" and "vanity," "rapture" and "strife," "earthquake" and "Victory" (28–30) became elements in a vicious circle ending finally in "The Victor overthrown! / The Arbiter of others' fate / A Supplicant for his own" (38–40).

While defining this warring dichotomy as inevitably destructive, and severely criticizing Napoleon for being trapped by it, the ode also begins to formulate (tentatively) a more productive kind of social participation, again illustrating the determining role played by the *conceptualization* of reality. In turning to Washington in the final lines (added after the initial draft was completed, at the request of Murray; see *BLJ* 4:104 and n), Byron points openly to a consideration implied throughout, namely that revolution becomes successful *only* when public life is understood to be identical with private life, and, conversely, when private life is understood to be identical with public life. Only when humanity is seen as a rich complexity of *all* experience can the crippling paradox of "guilty glory" (21, "Additional Stanzas") be resolved. The difficulty Byron had abiding by this conclusion is well known; to grasp the difficulty of even formulating it (particularly at this historical moment) we need only remind ourselves of its minority status in a period when individualist and idealist perspectives on social life were dominant.

The poems "From the French," written after Waterloo, restate this position, and also attempt to place Napoleon's accomplishments in a more positive historical perspective. In "Napoleon's Farewell," written from Napoleon's point of view, Byron would have the French general recognize that his failure did not result from revolutionary politics *per se,* but rather from his confusion of the necessarily *social* character of revolution with private desire: "I [Napoleon] have warred with a world which vanquished me only / When the meteor of Conquest allured me too far" (5–6). Even while admitting the travesty surrounding the Wars, however, Byron at the same time emphasizes the real and long-lasting gift that Napoleon, more than any other figure, brought to the modern world. Future revolutionary stirrings will be indebted to Napoleon as a model of possible achievement, even while his history offers a warning against wrong thinking: "There are links which must break in the chain that has bound us, / *Then* turn thee and call on the Chief of thy choice" (italics mine, 23–24)! Napoleon's statement here underscores the importance of strong leadership in revolution, calling attention to his own talents; but more importantly it stresses that such leadership *must* arise from public consent: it cannot survive in isolation from its

defining source. In the greatness of this lesson resides the hope and the possibility of eventual liberty. Rather than despair, then, there is cause for celebration, and cause to praise Napoleon as "My chief, my king, my friend" ("From the
French," 33):

> But let Freedom rejoice,
> With her heart in her voice;
> But, her hand on her sword,
> Doubly shall she be adored;
> France hath twice too well been taught
> The 'moral lesson' dearly bought—
> Her Safety sits not on a throne,
> With CAPET or NAPOLEON!
> But in equal rights and laws,
> Hearts and hands in one great cause.
> .   .   .   .
> But the heart and the mind,
> And the voice of mankind,
> Shall arise in communion—
> And who shall resist that proud union?
> ("Ode from the French," 73–82, 91–94)

Apart from the continental conflict during these years, England itself experienced severe domestic turmoil, much of which Byron, by his own claims,
witnessed first hand, and much more of which he knew from conversation and
extensive reading. While in 1812 the British political system stood pretty much
as it had since 1688, and while most members of the aristocracy remained
blissfully unaware of the tremendous impact the dizzying swirl of events everywhere was making, sure changes were beginning to take place at the bedrock
level. Increasingly rioters and discontented citizens were from lower classes than
their perceived enemies; hence the growing hostility of government to popular
demonstration. But even more important than the fact of discontent was its
cause. If many middle-class intellectuals voiced social protest in the name of
liberty (as they understood it from Locke, Burke, and others), by far the greatest
single cause of rioting was food shortage, and the rioters were neither middle
class nor intellectuals, but laborers and nonworking poor. According to statistics
presented in A. D. Harvey's *Britain in the Early Nineteenth Century,* of the seven
hundred forty full-scale riots between 1790 and 1810, 335 (45%) were food riots.
In addition to rioting, oppressed groups relied upon secret letter campaigns to
make their demands known, sending out to strategic public points such caveats
as "Peace and Large Bread or a King without a Head." These and other
activities, Harvey states, "concerned specific aspects of lower-class life. They
were indicative of a fragmentized, partial consciousness," which slowly transformed the structure of British society.[28]

That Byron understood the politics of food is obvious. In numerous poems he stresses the horrors of starvation and also describes vividly ceremonies of feasting, emphatically associating political control and injustice with the distribution of food. To take only one example, "The Devil's Drive" (a satire charting Satan's tour through the economic, political, and social arenas of Europe and Britain) describes graphically early on "A child of Famine dying" (74), emphasizing "its hollow cheek, and eyes half shut" (73), as well as its helpless mother who is watching the child die. Later in the poem, Satan enters "a royal Ball" (193) in London society, where, amid the splendor and celebration, and in the presence of Madam de Staël, he becomes hungry:

> . . . he thought himself of eating;
> And began to cram from a plate of ham
> Wherewith a Page was retreating—
> Having nothing else to do (for 'the friends' each so near
> Had sold all their souls long before),
> As he swallowed down the bacon he wished himself a Jew
> For the sake of another crime more.
>
> (206–12)

While this doubtless is minor poetry, it is explicit social criticism, and it suggests the kinds of details in daily life Byron was attempting to address poetically. One could argue with little exaggeration on the basis of such scattered descriptions that in his view table manners, the eating habits of the well-to-do, were not so much a sign of sophistication and virtue as of oppression and villainy.

When discussing the state of affairs and the popular discontent of this period, an important point to bear in mind is that resistance, while occasionally strong, could not achieve the sort of real coherence it enjoyed later in the century (even, say, in 1820 or 1830) because, for one thing, there was no standard situation for the two million British working-class families. From one region to another, the literacy level, relative wealth, and working and living conditions varied greatly (see Harvey, 50–59). Even the London Corresponding Society, which had been most powerful in the 1790s, was not entirely a working-class organization. As government authorities noted, "it is most probable that it [the Society] must have been guided by persons of superior education and more cultivated talents" (quoted in Harvey, 53). One deterrent to collective consciousness, according to Harvey, was that "in the factories, the encouragement for the formation of a group consciousness, which might have seemed inseparable from the employment of large numbers of persons on single premises, was mitigated by the fact that a large proportion of the mill labour force was composed of children or women. In 1816, three-fifths of the labour in Manchester spinning factories was under 18 and probably a majority of the rest were women who even—perhaps especially—in the working classes had not been admitted to social organizational equality with their menfolk" (57). Protests and unrest were sufficiently numerous and violent to alarm the government, yet there were no real and binding programs or support groups to control the direction of political change.

The consequence, not surprisingly, was that a number of moneyed, educated, politically experienced individuals stepped in as reformists to make private use of a great untapped popular force. If the reform movements of the 1790s had been inspired by moral indignation at evident atrocities and by an apocalyptic vision of a better world, subsequent reformers, though sometimes earnest and upright (as in the case of Burdett), were often the worst of the political lot: "The impractical idealists [of the 1790s] had been replaced by opportunist dema-gogues" (Harvey, 221). After 1807, Parliament began to see an influx of reform-ers, many of whom (oddly) were more reactionary than progressive, motivated by a strong desire to restore at any cost the old nobility to its "rightful" place against the swelling middle-class tide. Harvey says of one such reformer: "Henry Clifford, the aristocratic Roman Catholic barrister, nephew of the fourth Lord Clifford, who was the most prominent lawyer amongst the reformers, was reputedly motivated by 'Impatience of the unjust disabilities under which his sect labours [which] had reconciled him to violent opinions in politics.' Clifford even denounced Pitt in open court for degrading the House of Lords, 'by inundating it with a crowd of low born persons devoid of talents or respectability' " (228–29). This is an extreme case, of course, but it is not isolated, and it illustrates an important element in reformist thought at the time. Further, even the more committed reformers such as Burdett and Cochrane served in a roundabout way to deflect mass solidarity, for by institutionalizing opposition they drained off whatever energy and coherence a broad popular movement might otherwise have hoped for.[29]

That these social and political pressures directly influenced Byron is evident. His responsiveness to affairs of the day is attested specifically by his Parliamen-tary speeches as well as by his awkward, pained efforts to sort out his Rochdale affairs.[30] Perhaps even more significant, though more difficult to glimpse, was his inchoate awareness (which matured into decided revulsion after about 1820) that the conventional patrician attitude toward politics was severely limited by its desire to present "gifts" of liberty to the populace, without understanding that freedom from oppression is not a privilege but a right. His suspicion of most "progressive" aristocrats, with very few exceptions, suggests his feelings on this matter. Even Hobhouse was not exempt, as Byron could never be certain that his learned friend understood fully the social and political reality of liberty on its own terms, apart from the emotional and idealistic drives which usually accom-panied political enthusiasm.[31] For that matter, he could never be certain that his own analysis was sound, and when on occasion he felt that it was, he was unsure that he could conduct his life in accordance with it, and indeed he often contradicted his own statements about politics and society, expressing at dif-ferent times disdain for all political activity, cynicism about the possibility of social progress, and a strong desire to escape entirely the pressures of his immediate situation.

There can be little doubt, however, that when Byron returned to England in 1811 he felt no such confusion and in fact was certain that he could be politically effective *within* the existing British system. Although personal tragedy struck rapidly and savagely upon his arrival home (note, for instance, the deaths of his mother, 1 August 1811, and Charles Matthews, 3 August 1811), his determination was not broken. After these deaths he entered enthusiastically upon his intended political career as a studied, opinionated, and confident young Lord. That he abandoned his intentions after only three speeches, all presented within a four-month period, and plunged (at least so it seemed on the surface of things) headlong into debauchery and mindless poetry cannot be explained simply by the sudden popularity of *Childe Harold's Pilgrimage*. If anything, his popularity should have encouraged him in Parliament, for it gave him entrance to the most powerful and wealthy circles in England, including royalty, and this alone, had he exploited it, would have made him a potentially commanding political voice.

His failure resulted most immediately from his misreading and fundamental misunderstanding of the power and depth of the British political machine, particularly regarding its own estimation of its public role. At the risk of overstatement, one might venture that Byron was driven out of mainstream politics because his speeches were, in the eyes of Parliament, highly fantastic assessments of social reality. He had gone abroad to educate himself in the ways of the world, had returned home a cosmopolitan man (note the epigraph to *Childe Harold*), and had failed miserably in Parliament because education and cosmopolitanism were beside the point. Byron himself noted of his first speech that it "put the Ld. Chancellor [Lord Eldon] very much out of humour" (*BLJ* 2:167), though the extent and representativeness of Lord Eldon's response he did not understand; and Lord Holland, a friend and ostensible supporter, noted in his memoirs that Byron's speech was not "at all suited to our common notions of Parliamentary eloquence" (*BLJ* 2:167n). Day to day Parliamentary business, which always consisted first of preserving status quo power and opinion, even when considering progressive legislation, distorted the national and European context of politics and inevitably short-circuited any real efforts to change society. Byron learned this at his own political expense.

Byron's frame-breakers speech indicates very well his questionable merits as a potential Parliamentary leader and, further, provides valuable insight into the intellectual interests which he developed more abstractly (and evasively) in his poetry.[32] In arguing against capital punishment for frame-breaking, he stressed repeatedly that a simple law and order campaign, however strict, could not relieve a problem that arose from social circumstances and social relations rather than from innately vicious or criminal individuals. One major aim of his speech was to distinguish forcefully between purely individualist assessments of the riots and, in his view, a more plausible social perspective. To this end he made hunger the rallying point of his argument, accusing well-fed landowners, factory owners, and members of Parliament of remaining decidedly ignorant of its horror and prevalence, and of its power to determine the course of collective action. More than this, he darkened the picture of widespread British hunger by attributing it not to the laziness and general worthlessness of the suffering masses, but rather to the accepted economic system. Hunger, he argued, was not just a natural fact of human existence, but was produced by a set of decisions made without the consent of and without concern for those most affected; the populace were victims of a manufacturing enterprise which discarded and impoverished them and then *blamed* them, pushing them finally to a position where physical resistance was unavoidable: "These men never destroyed their looms till they were become useless, worse than useless; till they were become actual impediments to their exertions in obtaining their daily bread" (*LJ* 2:426).

This focus on the social and economic dimension of hunger suggests a related matter which Byron felt contributed to the increasingly difficult British situation. The labor system itself crippled laborers because it relied to an ever greater extent upon alienating principles and methods of manufacture (reflected most immediately in "the adoption of the large machinery" at a time when British goods sat "rotting in warehouses, without a prospect of exportation," *LJ* 2:426), thus destroying the integrity which comes from satisfying work. Drained of their enjoyment and of their sense of accomplishment, drained of their humanity, once proud workers turned against the very system that in better days their hands had built. Not *simply* hunger, but hunger reinforced by an irresponsible and exploitative economic system turned laborers into frame-breakers: "These men were willing to dig, but the spade was in other hands: . . . their own means of subsistence were cut off, all other employments pre-occupied" (*LJ* 2:426).

A further aim of this speech was to argue that Britain's frame-breaking episode was integrally bound to the international situation, that is, to the fact that England was fighting an unpopular war with no end in sight: "When we are told that these men [the frame-breakers] are leagued together not only for the destruction of their own comfort, but of their very means of subsistence, can we forget that it is the bitter policy, the destructive warfare of the last eighteen years, which has destroyed their comfort, your comfort, all men's comfort" (*LJ* 2:426)? But Byron wanted to do more than simply note that domestic issues, including the frame-breaking problem, inevitably are influenced by war. He wished to stress as well that international affairs can actually be used to obscure domestic social relations and thus (at least indirectly) to excuse and even to promote unjust domestic policies. He gives as an example of this the widespread British support of the Portuguese after the French had destroyed their country. British energies and monies were expended readily on worthwhile neighbors who wished to build a strong social system, even while Britain itself suffered "a starving population" (*LJ* 2:428). The effect of Britain's international humanitarian gestures, of course, was to shift the moral burden away from its own local atrocities, absolving itself of what went on at home by being extraordinarily helpful abroad. Byron's outrage at such political posturing is stated explicitly: "I have traversed the seat of war in the Peninsula, I have been in some of the most oppressed provinces of Turkey; but never under the most despotic infidel governments did I behold such squalid wretchedness as I have seen since my return in the very heart of a Christian country" (*LJ* 2:429).

Byron's emphasis on hunger, labor, alienation, and domestic and international contexts constitutes a sharp and intelligent criticism of British policymaking. Parliament, he believed, would pass laws without "previous inquiry" or "deliberation," would "sign death-warrants blindfold" (*LJ* 2:427). The only sure way to solve a problem, however, is to understand precisely what makes it a problem, and this requires examination not only of its explicit physical manifestations (i.e., workers destroying the looms), but more importantly of its various social and ideological dimensions. To this end Byron insisted that local hunger and violence, powerful as they were in themselves, could not be understood or effectively addressed apart from national economic policies and international war policies. Only by *opening* the field of social inquiry and subjecting the English system to rigorous examination could "conciliation" occur (*LJ* 2:427) or problems be resolved. To address a problem with sheer unadulterated force, without the benefit of intellectual flexibility, was not only ineffective as a solution; most often it would exacerbate matters. Byron defiantly asked his peers: "Can you commit a whole country to their own prisons? Will you erect a gibbet in every field, and hang up men like scarecrows? . . . Are these remedies for a starving and desperate populace? Will the famished wretch who has braved your bayonets be appalled by your gibbets" (*LJ* 2:429)?

If this speech teaches us anything about Byron's intellectual perspective it is that he refused to string facts together to produce predetermined conclusions (for instance, frame-breakers are villains, and their criminal activities are proof) and attempted instead to learn the structures, contexts, and *concepts* defining social reality. He rejected the violent proposal for dealing with the frame-breakers, not from a liberal "moral" position, nor from an idealization of working people; his position rested upon his belief that violence would not work because it addressed a symptom of a problem rather than the problem itself. His speech on Catholic Emancipation and (to a lesser degree) his presentation of Cartwright's petition for reform illustrate this same tendency to look beneath surface manifestations to the economic, political, and ideological determinants of social life. In speaking on the Catholic question, he understood and stated openly that some had become "enriched with the spoils of their ancestors" (*LJ* 2:435), and that present exploiters absolved themselves of this dirty fact by believing that the majority of Catholics "have nothing more to require" (*LJ* 2:432). Persecution took place under a system of values which redefined social fact in such a way that oppression *appeared* not to exist. Further, as in his frame-breakers speech, he stressed that only a positive and flexible approach to social problems could in fact solve them and lay the groundwork for prosperity, while continued oppression would surely destroy even the oppressors themselves by providing a building block for international tyranny (i.e., by establishing tyranny as a "natural" fact of life). As should be apparent, his speeches on behalf of victimized groups do not reflect his belief in blind toleration of all perspectives, as the stereotypical liberal position might, nor do they simply reflect his abstract cynical view of the British political system; they are founded upon his serious commitment to defining issues historically, that is, to locating them as completely as possible amid material circumstances in the objective world of action. This alone could provide a valid basis for judgment and commitment.

Byron's defense of the Catholics and his references to Christianity in his frame-breakers speech graphically illustrate the political light in which he had come to view religion, encouraging us to consider anew his so-called "atheism," "skepticism," and hatred of cant that scholars often note. It is important to understand that Byron never belittled individuals for their sincere religious commitments, whether they were Catholics, Jews, or Methodists;[33] his negative remarks were directed at the public role religion played in shaping and governing human thought and conduct, and at those people who exploited that role. From this perspective, the question of his atheism is irrelevant, and discussions of his hatred of cant are too abstract and too mechanical to serve much purpose. To dwell upon whether God exists, or upon whether an individual abides sufficiently by his creed, is to cast the religious question in reductive terms that ignore what religion *does* in the world of human experience. The briefest glimpse at his letters addressing religion, particularly his letters to Hodgson, shows that his thinking here follows the same lines of thought examined above. In August and September 1811 he wrote several letters to Hodgson about religion. In some he adopted a cynical, scoffing attitude ("what nonsense it is to talk of Soul, when a cloud makes it *melancholy,* & wine—*mad,*" BLJ 2:95), but in at least one letter he spoke his mind energetically and angrily, revealing in the heat of the moment convictions which changed very little over the years. As this letter is crucial not only to the tales, but also to much that he wrote subsequently, I shall quote it at length:

One remark and I have done: the basis of your religion is *injustice;* the *Son of God,* the *pure,* the *immaculate,* the *innocent,* is sacrificed for the *guilty.* This proves *His* heroism; but no more does away with *man's* guilt than a schoolboy's volunteering to be flogged for another would exculpate the dunce from negligence, or preserve him from the rod. You degrade the Creator, in the first place, by making Him a begetter of children; and in the next you convert Him into a tyrant over an immaculate and injured Being, who is sent into existence to suffer death for the benefit of some millions of scoundrels, who, after all, seem as likely to be damned as ever. As to miracles, I agree with Hume that it is more probable men should *lie* or be *deceived,* than that things out of the course of nature should so happen. Mahomet wrought miracles, Brothers the prophet had *proselytes*, and so would Breslau the conjurer, had he lived in the time of Tiberius. Besides, I trust that God is not a *Jew*, but the God of all mankind; and, as you allow that a virtuous Gentile may be saved, you do away the necessity of being a Jew or a Christian. I do not believe in any revealed religion, because no religion is revealed; and if it pleases the Church to damn me for not allowing a *nonentity*, I throw myself on the mercy of the '*Great First Cause, least understood,*' who must do what is most proper; though I conceive He never made anything to be tortured in another life, whatever it may in this. I will neither read *pro* nor *con*. God would have made His will known without books, considering how very few could read them when Jesus of Nazareth lived, had it been His pleasure to ratify any peculiar mode of worship. As to your immortality, if people are to live, why die? And our carcases, which are to rise again, are they worth raising? I hope, if mine is, that I shall have a better *pair of legs* than I have moved on these two-and-twenty years, or I shall be sadly behind in the squeeze into Paradise. Did you ever read 'Malthus on Population?' If he be right, war and pestilence are our best friends, to save us from being eaten alive, in this 'best of all possible worlds.' I will write, read, and think no more; indeed, I do not wish to shock your prejudices by saying all I do think. Let us make the most of life, and leave dreams to Emmanuel Swedenborg. (*BLJ* 2:97–98)

The importance of these comments is not only that they stress the deep-rooted injustice of a religion predicated upon the sacrifice of innocence for guilt, nor only that they reject as irredeemably contradictory the concept of a benevolent God acting tyrannically against innocent creatures; the most telling point here is Byron's rejection, repeated twice, of *revealed* religion. The grounds for this rejection are that revelation removes the seat of values from actual human experience, assigning it an abstract, absolute, and ideal quality which unavoidably produces contradiction and ultimately horror when brought to bear upon history. To accept the orthodox Christian scheme wholesale would be to accept a contradictory and tyrannical system of thought which would doom history to ever greater turmoil by making the highest values historically and hence humanly impossible. Rather than commit ourselves to "dreams," Byron says, a better way would be to commit ourselves to life, to *address* injustices rather than simply explain them as human inadequacy before some impenetrable and unknowable source. His position denies religious truth as it is traditionally conceived, emphasizing from first to last that values and moral principles make sense only within a human, social, historical context. Any system of thought that looks elsewhere for meaning, he says, works against human well-being. In these terms the question is not whether one is or is not a Christian, nor whether one believes in God, but rather whether one understands and is committed to life. If the commitment to life holds sway, as it did with Byron, then one is obligated to deal with its systems, of which religion is only one, determining their credibility by assessing them in a properly human context.

The issues and episodes sketched thus far certainly do not make a complete study of Byron's world during the Regency period. But they do begin to suggest, I believe, his earnest responsiveness to public life, and, further, to provide a suitable groundwork for considering his poetry in a broadly social context, including its conceptual and ideological dimensions. In tracing these various social concerns, I have attempted to establish two main points that have received little critical attention, especially with respect to Byron's early years. First, I have tried to show that the contradictions so often noted as deep-rooted in Byron's personality and poetry are most directly traceable to material and ideological contradictions at the center of British culture, and thus should be approached from a social and historical perspective rather than, say, from a purely psychological one. This is not to deny the active subjective power of Byron's imagination, but rather to stress that its character is conditioned by and contained within a larger, encompasssing social world. Second, I have argued that Byron responded to certain pressures by attempting to conceptualize or theorize about social life, that is, by attempting to develop a critical awareness of those elements which determine the structures of human experience. His conviction, though not always elaborated clearly or pursued rigorously, was that these structures must be defined historically and socially rather than abstractly or idealistically. As G. Wilson Knight stated more than thirty years ago: Byron "possessed, from the start, the *will* towards a comprehensive historical understanding."[34]

I now wish to examine the Eastern Tales at some length in an attempt to document specific ways that Byron formulates poetically the social pressures with which he contended. In turning here exclusively to the poetry, however, I do not wish to relegate society to "background" interest, nor to treat the tales abstractly. My aim is to build upon the previously sketched material, allowing the poems to throw the rich detail of social life into relief, to magnify rather than obscure its active role. In this way, I hope, the social dimension of the poetry can be more fully understood.

2

The Giaour

WITH the exception of *Childe Harold's Pilgrimage*, *The Giaour* is probably the most difficult of Byron's poems to discuss satisfactorily, not simply because it is excessively melodramatic and overtly escapist, nor even because in its final form it remains disturbingly fragmented. The difficulty arises because, like *Childe Harold*, the poem is extremely vulnerable to an array of both obvious and submerged influences (personal and public) which are effectively transformed through the course of the narrative into abstract "Byronic" characteristics. By taking advantage of the enormously popular Orient (and of his firsthand knowledge of it),[1] by exploiting certain personality features that had been prominent and successful in *Childe Harold*, and by planting his intellectual confusions within a literary framework of piecemeal storytelling (in the fashion, say, of Rogers's *The Voyage of Columbus*), Byron turns reader attention almost entirely to the poem's fictive and personal ingredients. These emphases tend to reduce the poem's flexibility, so that deep-seated psychological confusion or, at the other extreme, personal reflections on the eternal "human condition" seem to constitute its entire aesthetic dimension.[2]

One way of placing these purely literary and biographical interests in a larger and clarifying perspective is by considering seriously the role of the poem's prefatory Advertisement, which locates the narrative within a specific historical context. This brief note is important not because it insists that every recorded event in the poem should be viewed as precise or empirically verifiable (though, to be sure, Byron did remark to Moore years later that his poem had "some foundation on facts" *BLJ* 9:80), but rather because it calls attention to the various social pressures which underpin the narrative, thus offering a helpful insight into the sort of world that Byron's characters inhabit. By setting the story shortly after the Russian invasion of Greece (1770), and precisely at the moment of Hassan Ghazi's campaign to "re-establish order in the Morea" (1779),[3] the Advertisement focuses two major considerations which together constitute the intellectual and political core of the poem. First, it reminds us that the action takes place amidst sweeping and momentous change, created not only by the bitter Greek struggle for independence against Venetian and Ottoman domination, but also by the pressure from Catherine II on Greece to pledge allegiance to Russia. Second, and closely related, it emphasizes that the specific historical moment of the story, rife with territorial dispute and plunder, and with savage military interventions, knew cruelty and violence on a scale "unparalleled even in the annals of the faithful" (BCPW 3:40).[4]

These historical considerations bear directly on the narrative action in several obvious ways. By stressing the disturbing social uncertainty impinging on every facet of personal and public life at the time the story is set, they provide an important justification for maintaining, for instance, that the religious and domestic tensions described in the poem are not purely psychological, but rather are conditioned by material circumstances which actively deny the possibility of human betterment. They also allow us to see that such episodes as the murder of Leila and the brutal assassination of Hassan are not necessarily isolated, arbitrary, and purely private acts, but rather are predictable incidents in a world pervaded by extreme violence. Likewise, they enable us to understand the Giaour's idealization of Leila as a desperate (if paradoxical) utopian gesture that attempts to combat this world by sheer force of will. In short, knowledge of the historical situation surrounding the story offers us a way of measuring many events in the poem which otherwise appear to be local and without social or intellectual content.

More importantly, these historical matters provide a necessary context for interpreting the ideas voiced in the eulogy on Greece and for understanding the significance of the eulogy to the narrative action. Far from being merely a set-piece, the eulogy (1–167) carries the imprint of the troubled situation described in the Advertisement, expressing powerfully the confused values of a world experiencing extreme turmoil. Perhaps the most compelling sign of deep-seated frustration and confusion generated by historical pressure is the notion introduced in the eulogy that the past and present somehow have become disconnected, and that the present lacks the purity, virtue, and valor that ostensibly existed in the past:

> Clime of the unforgotten brave!—
> Whose land from plain to mountain-cave
> Was Freedom's home or Glory's grave—
> Shrine of the mighty! can it be,
> That this is all remains of thee?
> Approach thou craven crouching slave—
> Say, is not this Thermopylae?
> These waters blue that round you lave
> Oh servile offspring of the free—
> Pronounce what sea, what shore is this?
>
> . . . .
>
> In vain might Liberty invoke
> The spirit to its bondage broke,
> Or raise the neck that courts the yoke.

(103–12, 161–63)

Such a view, while perhaps inspiring in its unbridled awe of earlier times, distorts historical reality and indeed may be said to constitute an ideology of lost greatness, that is, a value system capable of understanding human worth only within a context that in fact never existed and that hence cannot be recovered. In reshaping the past into an ideal landscape of human commitment and triumph, this position of course reflects dissatisfaction with the actual circumstances of the present; but, perhaps more importantly for the narrative, it also displays a reactionary belief that the present cannot be changed, and thus its idealistic impulse inevitably is accompanied by intense despair.

The encompassing belief in an absolute division between past and present involves a series of more limited or more narrowly defined matters that elaborate the tensions pervading the poem. In the eulogy, for instance, Byron stresses the division between man and nature that apparently has occurred over time, pointing out that, while human worth has diminished, the natural beauty of Greece has remained constant. But this change in humanity, according to the eulogy, has not resulted in man's simple alienation from nature; this is not simply a picture of static division, in which man is no longer compatible with nature. The process of man's degradation has transformed him into an aggressive antagonist against nature. If once "man was worthy of thy [Greece's] clime" (146) and was capable of achieving liberty and glory equal in worth to the beauties of the landscape, that time is past, and in present circumstances man "trample[s], brute-like, o'er each flower" (52). This notion, reminiscent, say, of Marvell's "The Mower against Gardens," is a fairly common and straightforward instance of an attitude that has been explored in detail in Raymond Williams's *The Country and the City*,[5] and it assumes, stated simply, that untarnished natural order, fraught with richness, virtue, and permanence is an ideal (in the same way that the past is ideal) which is no longer humanly accessible, and which indeed human intervention poisons. But, as Williams notes, such an idealized view of nature does not develop from an objective and accurate understanding of a beautiful landscape that unfortunately humanity has lost and now is destroying. The issue is traceable to the unsatisfactory conditions of the present, which is not idyllic, and it involves a process of displacement and abstraction whereby the ostensibly ideal landscape supplants real political and social relations as a source of value, effectively removing them from the stage of the scarred human imagination. Under the pressures of alienating material circumstances the landscape becomes a domain of utopian perfection that the human imagination would hold outside the destructive path of human history.

The tendency towards abstraction evidenced in Byron's descriptions of the Greek landscape not only makes optimistic human intervention into life increasingly difficult as actual conditions are written off as oppressive and impossible; it also promotes an emotional rather than an intellectual assessment of experience. Under these conditions historical thinking is lost, and explanations of human experience get attributed to "human nature," which is both nebulous and impenetrable. Thus according to the eulogy the Greek citizen has lost his

privileged place in idyllic nature not because the Venetians, Turks, and Russians
have taken turns mercilessly plundering Greece, but because he is instinctively
"enamour'd of distress" (50). Because of limitations built into his character man
could not retain and cannot reachieve the glorious stature which he imagines
was once his:

> It is as though the fiends prevail'd
> Against the seraphs they assail'd,
> And fix'd, on heavenly thrones, should dwell
> The freed inheritors of hell—
> So soft the scene, so form'd for joy,
> So curst the tyrants that destroy!
>
> (62–67)

By attributing man's present predicament to human nature, the eulogy colors
over the actual course of events that has created the Greek situation, internaliz-
ing material conflict and redefining it in psychological and naturalistic terms.
This concept of human nature systematically reduces reality to fixed categories,[6]
thus taking the possibility of human change out of human hands and replacing it
with abstract nostalgia and longing. In the eulogy the lost past is lamented, the
beauty of nature is victimized by human touch, and all hope of regained strength
is dashed—all value lies outside the grasp of human endeavor. Reduced to an
absolute and controlling reality of natural tendencies, humanity is trapped into
reproducing its own slavery.

One further matter, actually an extension of the previous idea, which elaborates the mental attitude governing the world of the poem can be mentioned
very briefly. This is the notion present in the eulogy that Greece, though
externally beautiful, is in reality dead: "Hers is the loveliness in death" (94).
While it is an Eden "of the eastern wave" (15), it is soulless and thus cannot offer
any hope of better life. The landscape in fact heightens for the viewer the
irredeemable doom that is thought to characterize the Greek people. And,
again, this attitude is presented in abstract rather than in historical terms,
attributing the death of Greece to its own internal shortcomings: ". . . no
foreign foe could quell / Thy soul, till from itself it fell" (138–39). This picture of
death and beauty shows explicitly the persistent self-destructive cycle that has
created a people who "now crawl from cradle to the grave" (150) and is self-
perpetuating, actually assuring ongoing helplessness. Because it is a cycle that
begins on the unquestioned assumption that moral worth and integrity are lost
or dead, it relegates the possibility of human triumph and liberty to insignifi-
cance.

The eulogy is integrally related to the remainder of the poem and in fact
provides a key to understanding its conceptual dimensions, for it offers a
projection or formulation of the troubling, oppressive, and divisive material

circumstances hinted in the Advertisement. We know from the beginning that certain powerful assumptions make a positive, celebratory narrative unlikely, and, further, we know precisely why—because the prevailing view of human life does not allow humanity's most cherished values into the actual public conditions of life. Moreover, the eulogy very effectively establishes these attitudes as universals, thus obscuring the conditions (sketched in the Advertisement) that underpin them. This process of mystification explains not only why characters in the poem cannot see beyond dominant patterns of thought to a more plausible social or historical analysis of experience, but also why these characters inevitably are drawn into hardship and destruction.

The complex characterization of the Giaour illustrates vividly the central importance of the ideas set down in the Advertisement and in the eulogy. The first and final descriptions of him emphasize his defiant rejection of the world and the extreme isolation to which such defiance relegates him. In the opening scene the fisherman-narrator describes him thundering headlong on horseback over the barren landscape, and the description makes him appear fundamentally detached from any collective human experience, and even from nature. The caverns and the sea are drawn upon in describing him (180–90), but only to emphasize his superiority to them. In fact, his passionate intensity and aloneness defy even time, so that there almost appears to be something eternal about him. In the brief moment when he suspends his hurried flight to survey the landscape and culture below him, he is presented as frozen, as a larger-than-life individual ready to explode under the pressure of internal tensions that no human or natural forces can appreciate or explain. In his more-than-human aspect, he is thought to be the embodiment of "Woe without name—or hope—or end" (276). In the poem's long final scene as well, when he enters a monastery, the Giaour is described as alone even in company, possessing a unique sensibility that is unfathomable, mysterious, and superior to the general lot of humanity. No one in the monastery knows his past (his "deeds"), his faith, his race, his feelings, or his beliefs, and his confession obscures rather than clarifies these. No one has any inroad into his character at all, even though in the monastery honesty and openness should prevail; and yet here as elsewhere he is deemed superior by his sheer mysteriousness and seeming distance from his situation. Even in death he remains an abstraction and a mystery, ostensibly removed from ordinary experience and from ordinary understanding:

> He pass'd—nor of his name and race
> Hath left a token or a trace,
> Save what the father must not say
> Who shrived him on his dying day;
> This broken tale was all we knew
> Of her he lov'd, or him he slew.
>
> (1329–34)

Such descriptions, which focus on the heroic aspect of the Giaour's character, operate through the entire poem, and they constitute a troubling mystification of experience and thought. That the Giaour stands alone, a completely isolated man who lets no one in on his secrets or motives, need not be understood as a sign of his strength or of his uniqueness. In a very real sense it is a sign of his entrapment in a world predicated upon division, a world which makes the connectedness or interrelatedness of experience difficult to perceive and to imagine as possible or even as desirable. In this view, his extreme aloofness, however much it is celebrated by the narrators of his story, is a reflection of a completely privatized reality, and his defiance and criminal activities, as well as his commitment to Leila and withdrawal into the monastery, represent the horizon of possibility within a given social framework rather than the sheer imposition of his powerful will on some fixed external reality. In other words, alienation and abstraction are the conditions of his social life: they do not represent his superiority to it, even if the descriptions of him insist otherwise. Marx's comment about the inadequacy of viewing experience as simply private encounters with a static world makes this point explicit: ". . . private interest is itself already a socially determined interest, which can be achieved only within the conditions laid down by society and with the means provided by society. . . . It is the interest of private persons; but its content, as well as the form and means of its realization, is given by social conditions independent of all."[7] Thus the Giaour can only perceive and act upon that which already surrounds him; he cannot avoid it, even in the monastery, or magically overcome it. The condition of society itself (as evidenced, for instance, in the monastery scene, the Advertisement, and the eulogy) is one of division, in which reality seems to consist of independent, static, and discrete components. The Giaour does nothing more than provide a specific example of this social fact.

The understanding that the Giaour represents a living portion of a specific social reality, and that he does not in any way stand apart from the world he inhabits, illuminates other important aspects of the narrative, particularly the love relationship between Leila and the Giaour. Byron here, as in other poems, perhaps takes unfair advantage of his female character (a problem that he will address directly in *The Cosair* and in several later works, for instance *The Two Foscari*), treating her as entirely passive and as a reward for or object of devotion for men. But in handling Leila in this way, he is doing no more than making her character historically accurate; to have created her differently would have violated the social world of the poem. Further, even if the narrative portrays Leila in stereotypically one-dimensional fashion, as the woman every man dreams of, it does not so much celebrate her shallowness and passivity as defend her integrity and humanity against a social norm that as a matter of course victimizes women. This becomes clear if we consider not simply the Giaour's adoration of the beatific Leila, but also the desperate struggle between two violently cruel men who wish to *dominate* her absolutely: Hassan possesses her physical being; the

Giaour (according to his own accounts) possesses her affections. The narrative, by sheer reduction of Leila to such an extreme position, powerfully displays widely held social assumptions that are taken as universal truths and offers a compelling critique of how social injustice is often sanctioned by systems of belief that define self-interested acts and rites as "natural."

That Leila is not allowed human dimensions, but rather is projected as an ideal form, is stressed through the entire narrative, in the scenes both before and after her death, and this alone would suggest the extent of the Giaour's alienation as well as the powerful ability of social codes to confuse specific human situations. Leila is not perceived simply as ethically superior to other people, but as qualitatively different from them, as though she belonged entirely to another realm of experience, toward which humanity has always aspired. She is a "Soul" (477, 480), perfect and pure, and as the fisherman states:

> . . . should our prophet say
> That form was nought but breathing clay,
> By Alla! I would answer nay;
> Though on Al-Sirat's arch I stood,
> Which totters o'er the fiery flood,
> With Paradise within my view,
> And all his Houris beckoning through.
> Oh, who young Leila's glance could read
> And keep that portion of his creed,
> Which saith that woman is but dust,
> A soulless toy for tyrant's lust?
>
> (480–90)

And by the Giaour, Leila, even after her death, is viewed as "a form of life and light" (1127), and the love she inspires is seen as a

> . . . light from heaven—
> A spark of that immortal fire
> With angels shar'd—by Alla given
> To lift from earth our low desire.
>
> (1131–34)

These encomiums tell more about the Giaour than about Leila, and specifically they indicate the extent to which he has come to believe that nothing in ordinary human experience any longer carries meaning. Even the one relationship, love, which might be understood as a last, private refuge against the hopelessly cruel world that has alienated him, is entirely abstracted, transformed into a spiritual ideal stripped of all its human features. In his adoration of Leila, the Giaour never speaks in terms of actual human exchanges and relationships, but always in terms of his dream of what life might or should be, and he invests this dream with the meaning and importance that he cannot find in everyday experience. With his most fundamental needs unmet, his desires become up-rooted from social reality and are directed to an idea that he believes is more fundamental and valuable than mere life.

What the Giaour cannot see is that this commitment to what he believes is an overriding and absolute ideal in reality tightens the control of existing condi-tions over him. By accepting at face value the priority of form over life, by denying that the material world has any redeeming worth, and by investing all of his imagination and moral energies in a private *vision* of woman, he effectively removes himself from the realm of actual possibility, thus assuring that existing religious, political, economic, and moral structures will remain unchanged (despite the assassination of Hassan) to continue their tyranny over human life. The nature of his commitment to Leila narrows the sphere of human interven-tion into life to the point where human action is entirely private and where self-annihilation is thus inevitable.

A further, rather different, point about the Giaour's idealization of Leila bears stressing. If his all-consuming love traps him into a private and then finally into an essentially passive role, evidenced most clearly by his withdrawal into the monastery, it also serves as a commentary on the oppressive conditions of his existence. His utopianism (i.e., his idealization of Leila) betrays a deep human need that is not met by present circumstances. Viewed in this way, the idealized Leila is not simply a fantasy that the male ego has created, nor a never-never land of desire for which humanity eternally longs, but a symptom of specific and severe ills, and a sign of hope that these ills can be dealt with. The Christian and Moslem faiths, the political authority represented by Hassan, the accepted domestic relationships (again represented by Hassan), the unquestioned rules of power, economics, and social stratification—none of these alone or collectively provides a satisfactory context for meaningful commitment. Hopeless of material improvement, the Giaour thus looks elsewhere (to Leila) for fulfillment. Escap-ism, idealism, utopianism all are traceable back, once again, to the network of social relations that prevail in the Giaour's world. As M. I. Finley notes (writing in a different context), they "grow out of the society to which they are a response," and thus they suggest a sort of yielding to extreme pressure.[8]

This of course is not to say that the Giaour's escapist and utopian longings are admirable, nor is it to gloss over the human atrocities for which the Giaour is responsible; it is simply to stress that the disproportion between his idealization of Leila and the actual conditions of the world he moves about in is one measure of the poem's social context. The specific way his utopianism is manifested provides additional insight into the system of belief, not very attractive, that prevails in his world. That the Giaour must dominate Leila, that he redefines her human character in explicitly nonhuman terms so that she represents for him ideal rather than human worth, is not a sign of his virtue, but a sign of his desperation, a suggestion that if she fails him then his life is worthless (which of course is precisely the conclusion toward which the narrative moves). In addition, his idealization of her displays vividly a fundamental contradiction at the center of the system of ideas inscribed in the poem, clarifying further the inconsistencies evident in other parts of the narrative. Leila represents for the Giaour spiritual purity, and yet he conducts himself absolutely selfishly and ruthlessly in displaying his commitment to her. It becomes apparent through the narrative that her value for him depends exactly on his ability to take her for himself from Hassan and to possess her entirely. In searching for his own humanity, he denies hers. Worse, although she is for him pure and angelic, he claims that, had she betrayed him as she did Hassan, he (like Hassan) would have destroyed her:

> Yet did he [Hassan] but what I had done
> Had she been false to more than one;
> Faithless to him—he gave the blow,
> But true to me—I laid him low;
> Howe'er deserv'd her doom might be,
> Her treachery was truth to me.
>
> (1062–67)

Clearly there are difficulties here which cannot be explained satisfactorily in terms of love, personal relationships, or even abstract longing. Leila is made to embody different and contradictory values: she is pure in so far as she is a slave; she is worth loving in so far as she is not a woman; she represents values of the highest degree in so far as the Giaour possesses her; she is true to him in so far as she betrays Hassan. The Giaour's position here reveals a culture and a character so divided that only private meaning is imaginable, and this, through its sheer narrowness and selfishness, jeopardizes, threatens, and compromises all social possibility and finally all life. The Giaour in his confusion is very similar to Emily Brontë's Heathcliff, who, shut out from meaningful social existence, sets about to construct his own private world with its strikingly private system of values. While his powerful individualism indeed displays the shortcomings of a corrupt world built upon class division and private ownership, it also destroys him and everything important to him because it does not constitute a viable alternative to existing conditions.[9]

The severe implications of these intellectual and emotional contradictions are expressly contained in the poem's portrayal of physical violence, especially in its presentation of Hassan's assassination. As in most of his poems, Byron here does not gloss over the details of physical violence, but in fact exploits them. In describing the Giaour's attack on Hassan, he emphasizes dripping swords, severed hands, split skulls—he presents the murder as a butchering act.

> With sabre shiver'd to the hilt,
> Yet dripping with the blood he spilt;

> Yet strain'd within the sever'd hand
> Which quivers round that faithless brand;
> His turban far behind him roll'd,
> And cleft in twain its firmest fold;
> His flowing robe by falchion torn,
> And crimson as those clouds of morn
> That streak'd with dusky red, portend
> The day shall have a stormy end;
> A strain on every bush that bore
> A fragment of his palampore,
> His breast with wounds unnumber'd riven,
> His back to earth, his face to heaven,
> Fall'n Hassan lies—his unclos'd eye
> Yet lowering on his enemy,
> As if the hour that seal'd his fate,
> Surviving left his quenchless hate;
> And o'er him bends that foe with brow
> As dark as his that bled below.
>
> (655–74)

If this is the most extreme instance of violence in the poem, it is not the only one. Other passages and scenes (including the Advertisement) establish violence as a way of life, as a commonplace occurrence that exists as part of a natural process of human experience (see, for instance, 67, 318–19, 374–87, 747–86). To glimpse this we need only note Hassan's murder of Leila, which the fisherman-narrator readily assists. This context of course does not excuse or even fully explain the Giaour's awful deed, but it begins to suggest the intensity of the pressures on him and the available means for addressing these pressures. The terrain on which he moves is determined for him by existing practices and beliefs. That he responds violently to his situation, therefore, should not be viewed as unusual; it is precisely the way Hassan responds and the way society operates. Although the Giaour believes that his violent life reflects the curse of Cain upon him (1058) and feels hopelessly trapped under its influence, Hassan views violence as an inescapable fact of life, and thus even in death betrays "no remorse" (1092) and no "Despair" (1094).

What makes the Giaour's situation unique is that, unlike Hassan, he cannot accept unquestioningly the code of conduct that sanctifies violence. It is true, as he says, that Hassan's "death sits lightly" (1073) with him, but it is also true that the death does not resolve or even lessen his dilemma, and that this fact sits heavily with him. In fact, the murder points up the inability of *any* personal action, however extreme, to change in any substantial way the world that he finds oppressive. The extent to which the assassination stands as an explicit example of his alienation becomes evident when it is compared to the murder

Hassan commits. Hassan's crime certainly is no less heinous than the Giaour's and in fact is in some ways worse as it entails the murder of a woman who is already a victim of society, and yet it is perceived as a matter of course, as a natural response under existing conditions. He simply binds Leila and tosses her into the sea, a virtually silent act, and then sets about finding a new wife so that he may continue his life. The Giaour, on the other hand, commits murder noisily, madly, desperately, experiencing fully every injury and atrocity that he inflicts. And even this, he realizes, proves nothing. He continues to bemoan the loss of Leila and to see his life as beyond hope. This difference shows at once the kind of conduct that usually goes unquestioned and at the same time its unbearable horror. The Giaour is no better and no worse than Hassan, but, as an outsider, as someone dissatisfied with the world he finds himself in, he provides an insight into the workings of social life which otherwise go unnoticed.

One consideration that illuminates the Giaour's confusion and develops the inadequacy and contradiction of the system of ideas motivating his conduct is that in murdering Hassan he achieves the exact reverse of his professed goals. According to his own comments, the Giaour is attracted to an idea and an ideal of absolute proportion which overrides and even transcends materially limited human existence; hence his identification of Leila in strictly nonhuman terms (1127–34). His attitude, however, involves a complete fact-value dichotomy that does not allow value to exist ultimately or fully within a context of material circumstance. To know the highest worth, his position suggests, it is necessary to overcome all merely human limitations. This view clarifies substantially the Giaour's thought and conduct, suggesting, first, that, as he cannot contemplate *pure* spirit, he seeks to dominate Leila and to redefine her entirely as a pure form which he can contemplate and worship. He invests his entire moral being in her angelic or nonhuman stature. In this sense, his noblest aspirations depend directly upon his ability to control and enslave Leila, to elevate her at the expense of her humanity into an ideal. Second, taken to its extreme limit, this attitude inevitably produces physical violence of the worst sort, for it is predicated upon the assumption that physical life is worthless and, worse, an actual impediment to virtue and thus must be defeated. The assassination of Hassan is much more than a simple act of revenge; it is a desperate act to destroy the obstacle that stands between the Giaour and abstract virtue. Even when the possibility of dominating Leila is removed by her death, the Giaour cannot see the inadequacy of his thought and continues to deny the value of human life by withdrawing into the monastery and into complete solitude, believing more than ever that his commitment to Leila is just and moral and that the murder of Hassan was appropriate. As he tells his confessor:

> I lov'd her, friar! nay, adored—
> But these are words that all can use—
> I prov'd it more in deed than word—

There's blood upon that dinted sword—
A stain its steel can never lose.

                                                    (1029–33)

In viewing Leila in this way, as an eternal presence, the Giaour denies the active
social conditions that have created her (as well as his perception of her), and
thus he never recognizes the awful exploitation and criminality in his position
towards her.

The pervasiveness of violence in the narrative also provides valuable insight
into the power structure controlling the Giaour's world. Physical violence is used
unhesitatingly as one means of containing and perpetuating existing social
conditions, specifically the power of the ruling class. The conflict between the
Giaour and Hassan perhaps confuses this point somewhat, because both are men
of rank and appear to be caught in a purely personal exchange in which political
and social considerations do not figure. In fact, however, the point of contention
is highly political, for the violent quarrel is over property (in the form of Leila)
whose "rightful" social place has become ambiguous. It is an internal quarrel,
that is, occurring entirely within a single social class, but is nonetheless political
for this. The disagreement between Hassan and the Giaour, intense and destructive as it is, does not represent a challenge to or a questioning of existing
controls; it simply illustrates the common means that the ruling class uses to
achieve its objectives.[10] This political dimension of violence is made explicit by
the fact that both men view resistance to existing controls as highly criminal.
Hassan murders Leila for her betrayal, and the Giaour, although he loves her,
agrees that her fate is warranted. Even if the Giaour's despair leads him to murder
Hassan and threatens to destroy the ruling class, he never questions the *right* of a
ruler to use whatever means necessary—including extermination—to secure his
power. It is in this sense that the poem projects a politics of violence, showing it
as a legitimate means of social control and as an acceptable ruling-class response
to controversy and dispute. From this perspective, violence is an issue whose
moral dimensions are determined entirely by social context.

The social conditions which implant violence as a way of life, at least among
the elite, also create a largely passive religious system to consume the otherwise
unbearable contradictions which threaten to destroy all order and meaning. The
long final scene in the monastery perhaps seems "rather pointless," as William
Marshall has remarked,[11] placed as it is incongruously against the earlier scenes
of love and violence; but in fact its placement reveals precisely its significance.
Religion is presented in the poem as a separate, disembodied set of values,
independent of the actual pressures of human existence. Although the Giaour
denies the *form* of religion, refusing prayer, communion, and sworn commitment
to the monastic order and Christian creed, he accepts quite readily the solitude
and refuge that it offers, because public life is no longer bearable. Though not
avowedly Christian, he believes that peace and especially "rest" (995) can be

found now only through religion, situated as it is (he believes) apart from the main currents of human experience. That his concern here is not simply or mainly physical comfort, but spiritual and emotional ease, is evident from his long, windy confession that details his every transgression. This confession does not bring him hope of paradise—which he is too broken to consider seriously anyway—but, as he admits, it allows him at least the "rest" (1270) he entered the monastery to find. His final reward is that his story wins his confessor's pity and humbles even himself so that, as he approaches death, he is calm, asking quietly for a simple Christian burial with only a cross placed on his grave. Violent as the Giaour's life has been, impious as he remains even in the monastery, disdainful though he is of all religious sincerity, he finally accepts the religious promise. Rejecting its form, he embraces and benefits from its function, which is to settle the disquiet of human experience.

While this view shows religion in a suitably favorable light, the poem at the same time offers a powerful understated critique of the social and historical role of conventional religion, illuminating its severe limitations and even dangers. The assumption that religious value is transhistorical and self-referential actually serves prevailing codes by obscuring their pervasiveness and power. In its very passivity it participates in and tacitly endorses social life as it is, indeed benefiting materially from ongoing turmoil. By offering only transcendental solutions to material problems it glosses over immediate human difficulties, redefining them abstractly and thus depoliticizing them so that they serve the ends of religion and, by implication, of social authority.

The Giaour's experience illustrates this point perfectly. He literally buys his way into the monastery (902–4), or, phrased differently, he buys his way out of a troubled and oppressive society, leaving the world which so disturbs him to continue its ugly course unthreatened by his presence. His departure from active social life does not relieve the violence evidenced in his personal experience, but, quite the reverse, admits that the conditions of that violence are insurmountable, and maintains that personal interest is thus the only valid concern in life. The religious alternative presented here, which focuses on private need, is, as it were, in Marx's words, "but the reflex of the real world,"[12] and is only apparently removed from social life by its abstract character; its system of values and beliefs is historically grounded in the circumstances that have driven the Giaour to distraction. To understand this reflexive quality of religion, we need only compare the abstract thought that the Giaour denies in the monastery with the abstract thought that he celebrates in his love for Leila. Though he rejects one and accepts the other, both are abstract, insistently transhistorical, and thus blind to the material base of human existence. Even if Byron does not chart direct violent results from the Giaour's monastic experience as he does from the Leila episode, he implies nonetheless that the situation is the same, that it is equally, or more, dangerous, that the monastery represents in institutional form that private impulse sketched in earlier scenes.

The poem's emphasis on division and atomization is brought into sharp focus by a consideration that has been implicit throughout this discussion—namely that, through every experience, in and out of the monastery, the Giaour's identity, like the Monster's in *Frankenstein,* remains unknown. Not only does he move through the story without a name; he never is given a religion, or even a race. The only clear identity comes in the Advertisement, where Byron notes that he is "a young Venetian," and in the monastery, where it is noted that "The close observer can espy / A noble soul, and lineage high" (868–69), a point which is also implied elsewhere by the Giaour's commanding presence, his military expertise, and his leadership role. The extremity of the Giaour's alien-ation and anonymity reveals the extent to which his perceptions and needs—rooted, as we have seen, in the social conditions surrounding him—have come into contradiction with those conditions. As Marx notes about alienation, " 'spectres', 'bonds', 'the higher being', 'concept', 'scruple', are merely idealist, speculative, mental expressions, the concepts apparently of the isolated individ-ual, the mere images of very empirical fetters and limitations."[13] This explains why the Giaour's devotion to Leila, fired by moral and spiritual longing, ul-timately produces violence, despair, and unhappiness. It is an isolated response to public conditions that reflects exactly the degree to which the Giaour has become enslaved by those conditions. It is not a sign of the tragic fate of man in some universal sense, even if the isolated Giaour can only comprehend it in this way. His alienation arises from the political, economic, religious, and cultural conflicts that underlie every action of the story and that, in turn, develop from the long history of difficulties sketched in the eulogy. His idealization of Leila governs his conduct. But this idealization, as a reflection of a divided world, cannot produce completeness of being; on the contrary, it must produce further division and isolation. This of course is precisely what happens through the narrative as the Giaour denies to an ever greater degree the claims of the world upon him, so that by the time of his death he is entirely stripped of any human dimension whatsoever, as Leila before him had been. In the end he is a mystery, a myth, a fragmented story. The cross which marks his grave suggests his alienation and suggests as well the encompassing idealization, mystery, and confusion enshrouding the entire culture.

A final comment on the accretions to *The Giaour* may help to unify the foregoing discussion and explain why the poem's social interests are so rich and varied. These accretions, which expanded the poem from a 344- to a 1334-line narrative, create its interpretative possibilities and indicate Byron's increasing sensitivity to social, historical, and political pressures. The original rough draft, which McGann describes in detail in his edition of Byron's poetry, includes almost no speculative material, focusing rather on the literal story of the Giaour, Hassan, and Leila. The accretions, however, delve almost desperately and certainly haphazardly into the contextual matters that charge events with meaning. Composed during the months of Byron's liaison with Lady Oxford, whose political influence was substantial, and immediately after that liaison, when he was becoming politically confused and apathetic and increasingly certain that a Parliamentary career would be impossible for him,[14] the accretions suggest the tremendous pressure on him at the time, showing his need and attempt to reassess the multidimensional character of all human action. The story he tells is simple, briefly presented; but its meanings, its points of reference, suggested in the nearly one thousand lines of additions, are as rich and elusive as history itself, manifesting themselves on every possible level, from the most simple and direct to the most abstract. While Parliament and conventional political life for the most part adopted a problem-solving attitude towards isolated matters as they arose, *The Giaour* moves towards structural analysis, that is, towards an examination and redefinition of issues and ideas within a broad theoretical framework.

I am not arguing that the poem is social theory in verse—it is more functional than theoretical—but that its technique and aesthetic impulse are characterized by their questioning and critical exploration of fundamental assumptions about social reality. No single response to an event, the poem suggests, can be adequate, for every event is simply one part of a much larger social dialectic. Thus, for instance, in its final accretions (1192–1217 and 832–915) the poem denies that religion can offer a real solution to human difficulties because it is, as suggested above, an idealized, transhistorical formulation that denies the priority of material life and thus leaves material conditions essentially unchanged. Although the accretions perhaps appear to add up to very little, as William Marshall has lamented,[15] in fact they are vitally important to the poem, for they provide the necessary, if crude, framework for placing and interpreting the social dimensions of the narrative.[16]

The Giaour holds a unique and important place in the Byron canon because, like *Childe Harold's Pilgrimage*, it is highly unsettled and unplanned, developed over months into poetic form by chance, produced under a variety of intense pressures and conditions. Thus it contains and exposes quite vividly the many turns of Byron's thought at this time and, further, suggests his need to come to terms imaginatively with the large and important attitudes and issues that governed his world. Rather than being, say, "rooted in evasion and a refusal to acknowledge human conditions,"[17] the tale is committed in its idiosyncratic manner to exposing specific human realities, denying only that an abstractly conceived human condition can offer much insight into actual affairs. It is not so much "man's eternal predicament on earth"[18] that is at issue in the poem as the specific difficulties of living under oppressive, historically generated conditions that make love and all positive human relations impossible. While the tale is gloomy, riddled with pessimism, it presents its gloom and pessimism through the facts of violence, love, religion, and alienation that characterize the Giaour's world. If he dies of lost love and unhappiness, believing that only unattainable ideals have any value, it is because he has inherited a limiting and contradictory system of ideas and beliefs and not because human life is naturally and forever doomed to this fate. *The Giaour,* for all its faults, is a critical and inquiring poem; it examines and challenges the assumptions about human experience that often go unquestioned or that are believed to be absolute and unchanging. In this way the poem marks a substantial contribution to Byron's social vision.

3

The Bride of Abydos

BYRON was even more apprehensive about the merit of *The Bride of Abydos* than he had been about previous works. He seems to have been particularly worried about specific, even minor, inconsistencies in the poem, fearful that errors of fact or detail might expose more substantial weaknesses. For instance, he lamented his blunder in titling the poem *The Bride* when in fact no bride exists in the story. Although he occasionally attempted to gloss over the matter by insisting that "bride" could refer to one who is betrothed as well as to one newly married, in truth he was quite bothered, seeing this as a sign that the entire poem was a failure. As he noted despondently of the tale in his journal: "It can't be good, or I should not have stumbled over the threshold, and blundered in my very title" (*BLJ* 3:233). His anxiety reached its highest pitch when the tale found its way in manuscript into Gifford's hands, who reviewed it for Murray. Byron wrote Gifford a self-pitying and self-deprecatory letter to apologize and to explain that the poem "was written—I cannot say for amusement nor 'obliged by hunger and request for friends' but in a state of mind from circumstances which occasionally occur to 'us youth' that rendered it necessary for me to apply my mind to something—any thing but reality—and under this not very brilliant inspiration it was composed" (*BLJ* 3:161). He then concluded on a self-consciously humorous note by remarking that "I promise never to trouble you again under forty cantos and a voyage between each" (*BLJ* 3:162). Here as elsewhere he nervously explained the poem by admitting its weaknesses and then by insisting that it was written hurriedly (in four nights, he says at one point [*BLJ* 3:208]) to meet private needs which were more important to him at the time of composition than either aesthetic considerations or hopes of popularity.

His impulse to explain and to apologize for the poem, and his sensitivity about the poem both before and after friends read it, suggest that he had made an important personal investment in it. As his remarks make clear, the story conveys ideas and feelings that were close to him and about which he was not very confident. The immediate circumstance that inspired the poem was of course his deep involvement at this time with his half-sister, Augusta, and his unusual sensitivity, defensiveness, and embarrassment about *The Bride* usually are traced to this episode. Leslie Marchand, who has studied the incestuous affair in detail, remarkes that "the sense that he [Byron] was fated to succumb to a love that had 'something of the terrible' in it is reflected very clearly in the Oriental tales in which he poured out the 'lava' of his inner conflicts." And Byron, especially while writing *The Bride*, Marchand says, had Augusta "very much in his mind."[1]

While this affair doubtless has a very important bearing on Byron's thought and writing, occupying him to the point of distraction, it constitutes only a part of his experience at this time, and cannot explain fully the various levels on which *The Bride* works. The poem embodies and projects much more than simply his private confusions, however tormenting these may have been. The intense pressure he was under due to this unconventional liaison was accompanied by his growing apathy and confusion in the months following his affair with Lady Oxford, particularly with respect to public commitments. As he noted in his journal about his dwindling political involvements, "If I had any views in this country, they would probably be parliamentary. But I have no ambition; at least, if any, it would be 'aut Caesar aut nihil'" (*BLJ* 3:217). His private sexual affairs were no more compelling or formative than these anxieties. Moreover, during the latter months of 1813 his personal feelings were often voiced in the context of public issues, presented against a broad background of social interest. In fact, his personal difficulties seem to have made him increasingly sensitive to the interconnections between personal and public life. Especially in his journal entries immediately surrounding the composition of *The Bride* he displays a sincere effort to sort through those affairs that were both close to home and of a national and international nature, jotting down ideas about politics, psychology, aesthetics, and history, as well as personal life. He ventures remarks on subjects ranging from Newton to Wordsworth, often contradicting himself but always returning to the issue of finding one's way in (or out of) society.

To glance at his allusions and comments in his journal for November 1813 (the month of *The Bride*'s composition) is to realize the extensiveness and intensity of Byron's social, historical, and aesthetic concerns even while he appeared most absorbed in private, exotic, and escapist scribblings. In his very first entry in the journal, the same entry which notes his completion of *The Bride* (14 November 1813), he states offhandedly and sardonically that "I begin to believe with the good old Magi, that one should only pray for the nation and not for the individual;—but, on my principle, this would not be very patriotic" (*BLJ* 3:205). This implicit criticism of individualism, though it is immediately disavowed by his recollection of patriotism, comes at a time when Byron himself was displaying his strongest Byronic side to the public and creating Byronism as a dominant feature of his poetry as well, suggesting (at the very least) that, despite his conscious, even self-conscious, presentation of himself as his own defiant hero, he was aware on some level that issues could not be addressed effectively in purely individualistic terms. In fact, at every stage his Byronism is countered by his interest in the inner workings of social life. In the journal he offers reflections on Napoleon, makes passing allusions to Cobbett, calls up bits of public wisdom from Gentleman Jackson ("Whoever is not for you is against you," *BLJ* 3:213), speculates on the nature of wealth and revolution, ranks the living British poets according to popular opinion, and lists his encounters with Romilly, Mackintosh, and other reformers. Further, during this period he took every opportunity of studying the details of political and social life, as when he visited Hunt in prison (see *BLJ* 4:209–10, and n1 on 210). While his visit was a show of loyalty to the liberal cause (Hunt had been incarcerated for libelling the Prince Regent), it was also an occasion to consider directly what it meant to place oneself fully against a dominant power structure and, further, what it meant to be denied the ordinary rights of social exchange. After seeing Hunt, he noted in his journal that "though, for his own sake, I wish him out of prison, I like to study character in such situations" (*BLJ* 3:228). That such concerns remained important to him is evidenced by his continuing exploration of them in poetry after leaving England; *The Prisoner of Chillon, The Lament of Tasso,* and *The Prophecy of Dante* draw directly upon interests developed during the Regency years, considering in depth the social and psychological dimensions of incarceration, while other works, such as *The Two Foscari,* examine the subject in terms of the larger framework of social and political power.

His Byronic posturing notwithstanding, Byron situated himself (at least intellectually) squarely amidst the swirling and socially charged crosscurrents of his day and worked in his idiosyncratic manner to know and to systematize the world around him. The troubling reality he wished to escape through poetry was not simply a world of love and intrigue, but included as well the destabilizing war with France, the reactionary authority of the Prince Regent, and the mounting internal difficulties in Parliament, all of which combined to overwhelm him. That he could not face these matters directly, either publicly or in poetry, easily could have been a source of embarrassment to him as pressing as his sexual escapades, especially since virtually everyone he knew expected him to become a liberal political voice in Parliament. This is not to deny the significance of his private difficulties, but to suggest that they exist alongside other concerns and that these concerns achieve cohesiveness, if only briefly, in *The Bride.* Byron's loud denial of historical context in his poetry and his professed apathy, confusion, and cynicism do not mean that he was happily free of history, but, quite the contrary, suggest that he was directly subject to its powerful grip and that he saw no substantive way to come to terms with it. *The Bride,* as a plunge into mindless escapism, as an embarrassing personal anodyne for intense confusion and frustration, is motivated as much by social reality as by personal need, powerfully revealing the kinds of emotional pressures as well as the specific public pressures (power, violence, leadership, among others) that he faced and attempted to sort through.

In several important respects, *The Bride* marks a substantial advance over *The*

Giaour, both technically and conceptually. First, while its thematic focus more or less duplicates that of *The Giaour*, its formulation is much more coherent and precise. Not only does Byron appear confident in telling his story, however uncertain and apologetic he may have been about the likely reception of the poem; he also exercises admirable control over style and method, articulating more cogently and compellingly than before the subtle social dimensions of his narrative. Further, he develops a fairly consistent voice in the poem, a discernible and knowable point of view that is largely unimpeded by the emotional fluctuations which often plague both *Childe Harold's Pilgrimage* and *The Giaour*. [2] This development aids the reader significantly in analyzing the thematic layerings which undergird the story. These aesthetic and technical advances reflect Byron's growing ability to penetrate and articulate systematically a situation, problem, or set of ideas.

The Giaour, clumsy as it often is, anticipates this development. Though it began more or less as a rough story with virtually only anecdotal significance, the accretions reflect Byron's maturing understanding that narratives possess meanings, that there are ever-widening horizons of interpretation, and that it is possible to approach experience intellectually (as well as imaginatively) and to systematize apparently discrete and isolated events. This rush of accretions which utterly transformed *The Giaour* into stimulating and challenging poetry was followed almost immediately by *The Bride*, which shows the direct influence of its predecessor by formulating its interpretative, intellectual, and analytical components as an integral part of the aesthetic and imaginative process itself, rather than as an afterthought superimposed onto the poem. Hence the narrative technique and the interpretative thrust are less diffuse. This is not to say that the poem is entirely mature either aesthetically or conceptually. We must not forget Byron's own serious reservations, or that finally the poem is highly escapist, catering to the popular taste for diversion, reflecting the growing need of readers to be supported in their alienation by exotic and sensationalized versions of reality. [3] Still, in the context of Byron's thought and writing, *The Bride* constitutes an important breakthrough, suggesting with new force the aesthetic and intellectual potential Byron was attempting to develop and to master.

Perhaps the most important assumption taken over directly from *The Giaour* is that man and nature are fundamentally and forever divided, with nature possessing a purity that man can never hope to capture. In the very opening lines Byron focuses on the poem's setting, emphasizing its apparently abstract eternal qualities that abide somehow in complete removal from ordinary human experience. [4] It is a land characterized by flowers which "ever blossom" (1. 6), by "perfume" (1. 7), "gardens" (1. 8), the "fairest of fruit" (1. 9), "the nightingale" (1. 10), "beauty" (1. 12), and "virgins . . . soft as the roses" (1. 14). The only interruption of the otherwise perfect scene is man: ". . . all, save the spirit of man, is divine" (1. 15). Here, as in *The Giaour*, Byron plays man against his natural environment, implying that nature is transhistorical, an ideal model that forever stands as the goodness and beauty towards which man aspires, and at the same time as a measure of his repeated and inevitable failures. By projecting nature in this manner, as a desirable transhistorical domain, this early description establishes specifically the abstract attitude governing the narrative's social world and thus demonstrates immediately the obstacles to any substantive transforming action to which the characters may be moved. The description of man's relation to nature projects the ideological framework within which the characters operate, providing an important key to their understanding of all experience, whether religious, political, or personal.

Byron's return to this matter of man and nature suggests his need to address directly the commonly held Romantic assumption about the powers of nature. As one literary historian has remarked: "Nature unsullied by man was seen [by the Romantics] as full of spiritual value; and those peasants who lived in it (or the yeoman whose revival was so urgently sought) were believed to be spiritually superior to city men."[5] This of course is a generalization easily challenged by the fact that, for instance, the nature into which Coleridge's Ancient Mariner travels is not necessarily benevolent and perhaps is even sinister.[6] But scholars have found ways to explain even this,[7] and it is true that nature is idealized in much Romantic poetry. Keats's nightingale represents a beauty for which the poet desperately yearns; Shelley's Mont Blanc stuns the poet with its stillness and power; even Byron's Childe Harold, in the later cantos, occasionally finds himself overawed by natural beauty. But especially in the hands of Wordsworth nature takes on an encompassing, mythic significance to which Byron seems to have been keenly sensitive and resistant, perhaps because he believed that Wordsworth saw in nature a final solution to human difficulties, that is, an accessible refuge offering spiritual comfort to the deserving and properly pious individual. The story of Shelley's reading Wordsworth to Byron in 1816 is well known, and certainly in *Childe Harold's Pilgrimage* 3 Byron shows that his exposure to the older poet's work was important.[8] But long before this Byron had read Wordsworth seriously, though with little sympathy, and wrestled in his own writings with the ideas that dominated Wordsworth's poetry. For Wordsworth, in *Lyrical Ballads* and in *Poems in Two Volumes*, nature represents a permanently invigorating and value-laden domain which, through close observation and proper reverence, man can experience. As Geoffrey Hartman explains: "[N]ature, for Wordsworth, is not an 'object' but a presence and a power; a motion and a spirit; not something to be worshiped and consumed, but always a guide leading beyond itself."[9] While this idea is most clearly represented in *The Prelude*, a work which Byron did not know, it is also explicit, for instance, in "Tintern Abbey" and in the "Intimations" ode, poems which assume that under the auspices of nature one can be set free from the ruins of history and society. Nature is given symbolic proportions that overmaster the immediate conditions of human experience.

Byron doubtless never considered Wordsworth's nature in any deliberate philosophical or intellectual manner. Yet his own poetry details his inability to accept a position that maintains that personal and social life can be overcome or explained as a temporary or contributing stage in some larger benevolent scheme. By explicitly portraying Wordsworth's nature against his own controlling sense of society, Byron suggests that pure consciousness or transcendental redemption is not a self-evident matter. Further, he opens the field of inquiry respecting the connection between abstract thought (as manifested in Wordsworth's contemplation of mythic nature) and real social properties and expectations (as manifested in his own poetic characters).

Byron's poetry does not deny the existence of natural beauty, nor even that this beauty can provide moments of pleasure and fulfillment. Rather, it discovers and illustrates that nature cannot be abstracted from human experience, set apart as something fundamentally different from and superior to humanity, and that in fact such idealization often arises from oppressive social conditions. This point is illustrated early in *The Bride* when Selim describes his sojourn with Zuleika among the beauties of the surrounding countryside. Oppressed by Giaffir's authoritarian rule and disturbed by the terrible pressures of their duty to the state, the young cousins escape for the evening into an Edenic realm where "earth, main, and heaven [were made] our own!" (1. 70). For a moment they dream that all the world lies before them, that theirs is the experience contained in "Mejnoun's tale, or Sadi's song" (1. 72), and that, like Arnold's lovers in "The Buried Life," they know the rightful virtue and unity of their lives. They find relief in romance and in an idealized primitivism where freedom and vitality charge them with a sense of meaning and hope. That this is in fact, however, idle dreaming, motivated by something other than the inherent truth and allure of their dreams, is obvious; they never really penetrate Giaffir's stern rule, never overcome their intense alienation, never find more than a moment's pleasure (even though they belong to the highest social class). Their stolen moments alone in the beautiful evening landscape are a direct response to the unhappiness they experience in their daily lives. "The fairest scenes of land and deep" (1. 60) are attractive as relief from "my duty" (1. 75) to a "despot" (1. 45).

In this view, nature, like Selim, is not what it appears; it is an imagined land of happiness untouched by hardship, much as the moors constitute a vitally alive domain for Cathy and Heathcliff in *Wuthering Heights,* or as the abandoned house constitutes a paradisiacal refuge from the world for the pursued Angel and Tess in *Tess of the d'Urbervilles.* Though it seems to represent a permanence and to promise utopian bliss, in fact it always gives way to actual human experience and involvement, betraying itself as merely a dream of what *should* be rather than as an example of what *is* in the world as it presently exists; it is an abstraction of life rather than life itself, determined at every point by the reality of events. [10] Byron illustrates this point vividly in the final scenes of the tale, when the beautiful evening landscape that once had comforted Selim becomes the bloody battleground of his resistance and the place of his death. What began as paradise is finally riddled with violence and murder, and the belief that the world can be set aside, even briefly, in favor of a calm and superior landscape is shattered (2. 491–582).

The conditions which make nature appear to be a possible retreat from trouble and strife are inscribed everywhere in the narrative, and most explicitly in the physical structures of social life. The most obvious feature of the world being portrayed is the function of sheer physical power as a means of controlling the state and as a means of determining loyalty and individual dignity. Giaffir's right to rule is grounded firmly upon his ability to maintain and extend his power. He does not blink at the prospect of bloodshed ("We Moslem reck not much of blood," 1. 200), and in fact he understands the commitment to violence as a measure of one's private worth and social potential. Selim is ridiculed for his "feminine" distaste for a life of violence and is told that even physical resistance to Giaffir himself would be preferable to his present habit of withdrawing to "where babbling waters flow" to "watch unfolding roses blow" (1. 88–89).

The importance of one's capacity for violence and of one's willingness to assume power is reflected as well in Giaffir's choice of a husband for Zuleika. Osman Bey is described as a descendant of a noble line that is "Unchanged— unchangeable" (1. 202) in its superior quality, that is, in its traditional willing- ness to take up the sword to win and maintain power. To wed Zuleika to this man, Giaffir understands, would be to extend and to strengthen physically the controls of the existing state (1. 210–11), just as in a later work by Byron Werner's attempt to wed Ida to Ulric is intended to transform a potential enemy into an ally.[11] That Osman Bey's wealth is "ill-got" (1. 373) or that he is in fact descended from a "viler race" (1. 376), as Selim insists, is in political terms irrelevant; what matters is that his accomplishments are exemplary in status quo terms, and that he is committed to preserving the existing power structure.

Important as the willful exercise of power is, by itself it cannot account fully for the decisions and events that compose the narrative action. Individual strength and military coercion and repression are aspects of a complex and encompassing network of social relations, the most immediate and recognizable expression of submerged, extensive, and controlling processes of thought and belief that reflect, endorse, and define social life. They cannot by themselves explain how order endures, how it retains its mysterious strength over long periods, why an entire culture (despite occasional isolated objections) tolerates it and functions under it as though it were natural—in short, they cannot explain fully the social order within which the action takes place.

Although it appears that Giaffir exercises his authority personally and ar- bitrarily and that his control of physical resources alone enables him to maintain his position, in fact he could not single-handedly, nor even with the support of the military, control all of society if society did not consent. Specific social relations control the world of the poem and contribute to the build-up and concentration of power, both directly and indirectly, by openly sanctioning the strategies and modes of political conduct and, more subtly, by focusing social attention away from the larger structures of daily political life. Religious belief, for instance, undisguisedly endorses the spread of violence and exercise of power (see, again, 1. 200); personal life, as exemplifed in Selim's love for Zuleika, is perceived in terms separate from public life, so that full-scale political analysis and involvement appear to be qualitatively different from immediate personal concerns; work is structured so that slaves and peasants unquestioningly defer to their social superiors and so that wealth flows from the hands of labor to those who rule (see, for instance, 2. 20–23 and 2. 257–59); family life is the hand-maiden of political power, subservient to the demands of the state and hence supportive of those demands. While these issues are never given a prominent position in the plot, they are always present as the unstated assumptions and realities upon which the action is built. Every facet of human experience, in different ways and to different degrees, is mediated by prevailing social conditions and relations, and, consciously or not, contributes to the perpetuation (or ultimate destruction) of those conditions and relations by embodying and carrying out the values and expectations of the collective social order.

From this perspective, Giaffir is not an exception to political and social reality but an example of it. If he is a tyrant whose "Power sways but by division" (1. 434) and who earns the personal hatred of Selim, one unhappy individual, or even of several individuals like Selim, he is nonetheless the voice of those submerged realities upon which his culture rests, ruling not because he has overcome existing standards nor because he has shown his personal superiority to every other individual citizen but because he embodies and is able to maintain accepted public norms more fully than anyone else. In real political terms, this means that whether Selim is correct in identifying Giaffir as an assassin and a tyrant is considerably less significant than Giaffir's ability to uphold public order by assuring that dissent is perceived publicly as an abnormality, as a deviation from truth. That he is effective in this role is evidenced by the fact that, despite the personal question of his right to rule that has been raised and despite his seeming arrogation of all power to himself, he is defended by the social and political system against encroachments from the outside, even when the resistance comes from the son of a former ruler whom Giaffir himself through devious means has removed from power.

A further, related, point which bears stressing is that this ideological framework does not exist arbitrarily or as a neutral system, matter-of-factly supporting the tyrannical Giaffir or the next individual who happens to rise to power. The array of ideas and issues that combine into a comprehensive structure of social life has a very real source and direction, understood most fully in terms of class stratification. The threads of tradition, common belief, expectation, and conduct running through every facet of society reflect class domination, the issue which more than any other explains the unity and cohesiveness of culture.

When Giaffir exercises state power, he is acting as the protector and agent of class stratification, assuring social conformity and submission to class rather than to purely personal demands. The entire social fabric in fact, disparate and natural as it may appear, manifests the hegemonic power of the ruling class.

This class issue is implicit everywhere in the narrative. As a matter of course Byron establishes the ostensible rights and superiority of his main characters, including Giaffir, Selim, Zuleika, and Osman Bey, while never detailing the lives and personalities of ordinary citizens. While Giaffir is called a tyrant and Selim a slave, these characters, along with their peers, nonetheless assume their uniqueness in society and are described variously as proud, brave, powerful, beautiful, wealthy, richly clad, and ambitious. Played against these obviously privileged individuals is a vaguely hinted but nonetheless real class that is ruled over, consisting both of the slaves and the military, who work immediately under Giaffir, and of the peasants of the surrounding countryside, who produce the wealth of the nation that Giaffir uses to secure and extend his power.

The sheer limited presence of these latter people in the narrative action suggests their ordinariness, their conformity to established order, their willingness to live in the world as it is given to them. This is not to demean the populace for their ignorance and passivity, but to focus on the control exercised over them; they are squeezed out of the most pressing social and political concerns even while their existence makes all other accomplishments possible. They are virtually anonymous because the ruling class, for which Giaffir is the spokesman, controls not only the military, which is called upon periodically to suppress vocal internal resistance to the state, but also the quality of life, the character of belief, and the public perception of reality—in short, it controls both social practice and social consciousness. This power over every facet of public and private life makes the ruling elite appear to be homogeneous and immune to all political challenges. Although occasionally there are ruptures within this power structure, internal contradictions which appear to threaten ruling class domination, these are largely anomalous and are subsumed by the larger collective understanding of society as naturally and permanently ordered. And this understanding assures continued class division and class domination.[12]

The class issue helps to explain why Selim ends as a failed rebel. Although his resistance to tyranny may be heroic, at least on the surface, it is also naive, reflecting the mind of a self-indulgent petty antagonist who is unable to grasp the full significance of his situation. It is true, of course, that his resistance to Giaffir has been planned over a long period and that it has the potential support of a sizable band of discontented citizens who "only want a heart to lead, / A hand to point them to the deed" (2. 274–75); but it cannot be considered a truly political movement for it is too narrowly confined, motivated entirely by personal grievances, most immediately by his father's death and by his affair with Zuleika. He does not find "motive to be brave" (1. 362), for instance, until he learns that Zuleika is destined to marry Osman Bey. Only then does he begin to show himself as a different, braver, more masculine individual, casting aside his civilian dress in favor of pistols, a sabre, and golden armor (2. 131–50). His analysis of Giaffir's rise to power, his description of the exploited peasantry, his outrage at the criminality of Osman Bey, his defense of individual freedom: these may be accurate and commendable in their way, but ultimately they are hollow complaints that are never developed into a real, politically valid understanding of the systemic nature and class dimension of the events surrounding him. His decision to revolt, however moralistic it appears and however much it reveals the unsatisfactoriness of existing conditions, is reducible finally to his desire to substitute his own perspective and power for Giaffir's and does not constitute a viable alternative to existing conditions. Devoid of any far-reaching or substantial social potential, lacking broad popular support, his conspiracy remains a wholly isolated affair, reflecting at best his disturbing alienation from prevailing conditions; it cannot challenge seriously the state and social organization that Giaffir has at his disposal.

To understand the political insufficiency of Selim's position, it is helpful to compare his aspirations with Giaffir's rise to state power. Giaffir's story illuminates a further dimension of the narrative's political content by stressing the extent to which individual desires and objectives are always mediated by actual experience, by the network of social relations pervading every facet of life. While he was once an assassin, guilty even of fratricide, and while he displayed a near obsession with personal power, he was also a central participant in a politically tumultuous situation which over time had begun to weaken the structures of the ruling order. Fighting in league with his brother to defend the state against the powerful and determined rebel leader Paswan of Widdin who, as Byron remarks in a note, "for the last years of his life set the whole power of the Porte at defiance" (BCPW 3:440), Giaffir found himself the leader of a military band at a time when state leadership had long been under steady fire. He took advantage of this opportune moment by murdering his brother, thereby bringing additional soldiers under his own command, and then rode to power on his ability to win or buy broad support for his campaign. In time, "Paswan's feud [was] / In part suppress'd. . . , / Abdallah's Pachalick was gain'd" (2. 248–50), and Giaffir emerged from the turmoil as master and leader of the state, consolidating the disparate social and political forces under his authority. Unlike Selim, who is faced with comparatively quiet times, he found himself amidst volatile circumstances that created a sweeping desire for order and strong leadership and that thus made a serious political move for power possible. Whatever his private motives may have been, they could become determining factors only when the primary conditions of public life allowed.

That Selim never comes to terms with the encompassing role of circumstance, launching a conspiracy against the state at a socially unpropitious moment, causes him to adopt confusing and contradictory positions and ultimately traps him into a position that works against his interest and to Giaffir's advantage.

Absorbed by personal difficulties, perceiving his situation in purely individualistic terms, he fails to understand that in some quite important ways he
unknowingly remains loyal to the system he has rejected. That the existing social
values that Giaffir has unified and continues to defend actually control Selim's
thinking and help to defuse his planned insurrection, despite his professed
independence of mind, is exemplified in the portrayal of Zuleika, and particularly in the portrayal of Selim's relationship to her.

Byron was consciously experimenting in his characterization of Zuleika. As he
noted in a letter to Edward Clarke: "I . . . wished to try my hand on a female
character in Zuleika—& have endeavoured as far as ye. grossness of our masculine ideas will allow—to preserve her purity without impairing the ardour of
her attachment" (*BLJ* 3:199). Her importance is indicated by the poem's title,
which emphatically asserts that this is her story, not Selim's, even though the
narrative action seems to revolve mainly around him. As the focal concern in
the narrative, her role is very similar to Leila's in *The Giaour*. She is passive, one-
dimensional, the object of masculine dispute, and, most importantly, she is
consistently portrayed as an ideal who embodies the highest virtue, purity,
simplicity, and beauty to which the surrounding male characters can aspire. She
is introduced into the narrative as a "transcendent vision" (1. 162) who is "fair"
as the unfallen Eve (1. 158–60), "dazzling" as the beauties haunting Elysian
dreams (1. 162–65), "soft—as the memory of buried love" (1. 166), "pure—as
the prayer which Childhood wafts above" (1. 167). She is characterized entirely
in such terms, worshipped by her male counterparts for her "nameless charms"
(1. 177) and for "the light of love—[and] the purity of grace" (1. 178) that
distinguish her. That this is not simply a passing estimate, but the way she is
intended to be perceived in the story, is shown later when Selim, standing before
her in his rebel attire, describes her again as an ideal rising above the changes
and imperfections that long have plagued his experiences in a troubled world. To
him she is a "dove of peace" (2. 899), a "rainbow" (2. 881) that transcends and
dissolves all the hardships and struggles of everyday life.

Such descriptions as these help to explain why Byron's poetry more often than
not has been interpreted in psychological terms. To see only these idealizations,
or to see them as definitions rather than as symptoms or functions, leads
inevitably to broad statements about human desire, human need, and human
nature. Approached this way, Leila and Zuleika are the same, faceless and
interchangeable, important for what they tell us about *man's* eternal longing for
beauty and about the many perils accompanying the pursuit of this beauty. As
one critic employing a psychological approach has explained Leila's role in *The
Giaour*: "Byron proposes that the attainment of a love object inevitably brings
destruction to both the pursued and pursuer."[13] But such an account is incomplete, not only because it ignores the gender issue, unquestioningly accepting the notion that women are mere objects of masculine desire, but also because
it elides the contradictions, inconsistencies, and turmoil which underlie and

have given rise to the idealization and objectification of women; it makes its point by suppressing social reality.[14] With respect to Zuleika, if she is the focus of the narrative, as the title indicates, then to abstract her from the action (or to view her simply as the *object* of the action) is to flatten her into a hollow type, to obscure the *human* pressures and details that infuse her characterization, to overlook both the conditions and the effects of her status as an ideal. To be fully understood she must be placed within the context of action and ideas, approached in terms of the social, political, and historical conflicts which cause people to idealize her, rather than from the assumption that she is, *de facto*, an ideal.

The most important fact about Zuleika is that she is her father's daughter, a member of the ruling elite in a culture governed by authoritarian means. This would perhaps be a curious but still minor concern if she were portrayed as less perfect and pure, or if she felt alienated and oppressed under her father's iron hand, resisting in some substantive way his merciless power over her and the state. In fact, however, she is quite the reverse, actually displaying charm and sweetness that seem to approve both him and his political position, so that her characterization is made to have direct class implications:

> At one kind word those arms extending
> To clasp the neck of him [Giaffir] who blest
> His child caressing and carest,
> Zuleika came.   .   .   .   .
> Affection chained her to that heart.
>
> (1. 184–87, 191)

That she readily accepts the world as it has been given to her, loving Giaffir because he is her father and Selim because he is (ostensibly) her brother, suggests not only her youth and naivete, but more importantly the social relevance of her status as an ideal. The readiness with which she accepts her privileged position, the ease with which she moves in society, her willingness to follow prevailing codes unquestioningly, her acquiesence and silence in state matters—these, much more than simply her physical beauty and disarming grace, make her appear transcendently pure, the highest possible standard against which all conduct can be measured. Her apparently perfect nature is exemplified by the fact that, when Giaffir announces that she is to marry Osman Bey—a purely political move on Giaffir's part—she submits without objection even though she is disappointed.

What is projected in the narrative as an example of nonsocial and non-political purity is at every turn politically and socially operative, serving the ends of state power. Yet this is not due to Zuleika herself. She is the product of an aggressive masculine culture that depends for its survival on the continued subjection and submission of people. Through the ideological processes of this culture, she is manipulated, deprived of control over her will and her body, and then is given to understand that her powerlessness is in fact virtue, more laudable than the ugly business of politics. Made entirely passive, she fulfills the social role of women, becoming a repository of feeling and nebulous value, without real human dimension, who can be molded repeatedly to fit the aims and expectations of the ruling elite. She is, as it were, a perfect ruling-class example to society, the embodiment of qualities tailored to absorb contradictions and tensions which otherwise might create a restive and possibly insurrectionary public. In this respect, the very act of idealization, of elevating Zuleika above experience, is seriously political, an act of repression and deprivation disguised as reverence, with significance reaching deep into the social structure. To understand her role in this way is not to demean her, personally, as spineless, to suggest that she is consciously a party to tyranny, or to view her as something less than what she should be (under existing circumstances, which deny women any power and rights whatsoever, it would be difficult to imagine her as anything but submissive), but to emphasize that she does not so much transcend events as develop from them, and that she serves a very specific social function. That she is a woman idealized in a male-dominated culture, that she is denied her basic humanity and made to represent prevailing social standards of conduct and thought, reveals more about the actual processes of power and ideology than it does about abstract or eternal human desire.

Selim's relationship to Zuleika cannot be understood apart from these issues, for they illustrate plainly that his love for her is not only a personal act but also a social act, involving underlying and unquestioned assumptions about social life. Because Zuleika is connected directly and inextricably to the most fundamental principles unifying culture, for Selim to love her is for him to remain committed, at least on some deep, unconscious level, to the very system of beliefs that has alienated him and driven him to conspiracy against the state. This is not to say that his motives are insincere or hypocritical, or to suggest that they fail to demonstrate in some real way the oppressiveness of prevailing conditions, but to emphasize that social life is much more powerful and encompassing than either Zuleika or Selim realizes, that it pervades every inch of their beings despite Selim's insistent belief that certain matters are impervious to social reality. The degree to which existing controls continue to determine his attitudes and inform his most private decisions is seen in the fact that he does not actually love Zuleika for what she is, but rather for what he *thinks* she is, or for what he wants her to be (that is, transcendent and pure). Thus, as he prepares for combat he imagines that "all toils are sweet" (2. 452), because to him Zuleika is "the star that guides the wanderer" (2. 395), the symbol of good that will inspire him to win "the spoil of nations" (2. 413). He readily accepts, celebrates, and worships her, all the while believing that her beauty and virtue are attributable to a source outside society and specifically removed from the political establishment he seeks to overthrow. Although at one point he admits that "in time deceit may come / When cities cage us in a social home" (2. 436–37) and that "there even thy soul might err" (2. 438), he cannot entertain this possibility seriously and insists that there is ultimately an independent "world within our arms" (2. 453) which society will never control. He cannot understand her role in society nor grasp the full political significance of her affection, devotion, and love for Giaffir, Selim's own "deadliest foe" (2. 196). To perceive her as he does, that is, to overlook her very real social situation, to deny or to ignore her complacency under Giaffir's authority, does not constitute pure and noble love that overrides all circumstance, though Selim thinks it does, but, quite the contrary, suggests the powerful ability of particular ideological controls to resituate or divert real human issues into a different context, thus mystifying them. Though honestly motivated and illustrative of deep human needs, Selim's love for Zuleika is from the beginning misunderstood, an indication that Selim in fact has not broken from the existing social authority despite his contempt for tyranny and despite his brave realization that "life is hazard at the best" (2. 444) on the revolutionary front where new worlds are created.

The abstract thinking governing Selim's attitude towards Zuleika lures him into abusing her just as Giaffir does. Inspired by love and by an ideal of justice, Selim sets out to defeat tyranny, to win Zuleika away from her father, and to establish a peaceful world wherein he and Zuleika can live happily and productively together. Noble as his position may be, it is untenable because it denies the circumstantial priority and reality that infuse people and events with meaning, and because it is predicated upon a view of human experience as a purely private affair. In these terms, his struggle on Zuleika's behalf is not so much an attempt to offer her freedom, despite his assertions that this is his objective, as it is an attempt to mold her to fit his own personal dream of her. He believes that he can simply lift her, *as an ideal,* out of one social world and place her into another intact, as though she were devoid of any desire or mental and emotional capabilities of her own. He believes that after the battle, however thoroughly he butchers Giaffir, she will come to him as beautiful, as virtuous, as transcendently pure as ever. Her situation here closely parallels Leila's, showing the true sense in which she is an object. She is viewed literally as property over which two men dispute, one who claims the political right to control her and to assign her to her life-role, the other who claims to possess her affections. While it is noted in the story that Selim is her "all" (2. 636), it is clearly stated as well that she loves her father and is dutiful to him. These facts are suppressed by the larger and apparently more important political intrigue that is brewing, and thus her feelings go unconsulted; her importance lies solely in her role as possession, as the treasure to be won. Although Selim's motives are private while Giaffir's are political, both men are driven by ownership. In such a situation, the best Zuleika can hope for is to become Selim's possession rather than Giaffir's.

A second consequence of Selim's abstract thinking is that it leads him to commit the same acts of violence for which he detests Giaffir. When the military encounter finally develops, it quickly becomes an absurd, sad blood bath, producing a field of dead and dying soldiers. During the exchange Selim views around him "a gasping head, a quivering trunk" (2. 542), wild and confused fighting, terrible slaughter, men desperately trying to escape certain death. This violence exposes vividly the contradictions which from the beginning have been embedded in Selim's thought and character. It is true that secretly he has led a band of pirate rebels who have robbed and plundered to finance their eventual attack on the state. But, as Selim himself admits, he has not been a regular participant in these activities, and in fact for the most part his leadership has rested in his idealism, his strong heart, and in his organizational skills, rather than in his sword. As he explains to Zuleika: "I form the plan, decree the spoil, / 'Tis fit I oftener share the toil" (2. 476–77). The battle scene here tests his ideas against circumstance and represents his attempt to "prove all truth to thee [Zuleika]" (2. 306). Placing his values under the fire of direct experience, this scene illustrates the destructive potential of his position when it is pushed to the extreme.

His own violent death makes this point explicitly, for it comes precisely at the moment when his idealism and the pressures of experience collide. He is killed as he is moving away from society, the open sea before him, with Giaffir, Zuleika, and the world behind him:

> Ah! wherefore did he turn to look
> For her his eye but sought in vain?
> That pause—that fatal gaze he took—
> Hath doomed his death—or fixed his chain.
>
> (2. 563–66)

This is a very paradoxical moment. On the verge of breaking entirely from the world he detests, he pauses, frozen in a moment of fatal uncertainty between a world of lawful tyranny and lawless freedom, hoping to glimpse Zuleika once more, the ideal which alone gives his efforts meaning, but which, unknown to him, belongs entirely to the world he wishes to leave behind. At the moment of greatest crisis, when the world is on the verge of crushing him, she is nowhere to be found. That she does not cheer him on, that she is not even present, immobilizes him, makes him vulnerable, and opens the way to his violent death. At this moment, as nowhere else in the narrative, it becomes obvious that Zuleika simply cannot carry the burden that has been placed on her, and that Selim's view of her is dangerously mistaken—she is not independent of the bloody exchange between Selim and Giaffir, occupying some nebulous zone of pure value; she cannot preside over the murderous encounter between two people she loves as though she were the one disinterested constant in a mutable and violently charged world. Her withdrawal from the picture, leaving Selim to face combat alone, emphatically shows that, despite Selim's consuming love for her and despite his elevation of her to angelic heights, she is vitally and painfully connected to events, that the ideal she is made to represent cannot be transferred abstractly from one situation to another as though its value were universally applicable, and that ideals must dissolve under the intense and immediate pressures of actual experience. Further, it becomes clear that denial of these facts is unavoidably destructive, whether it is a tyrant such as Giaffir or a sensitive loner such as Selim who celebrates an image of life over life itself. In this view, Selim's death scene is not so much a matter of love getting in the way of action (it is not an example of uxoriousness, wherein Selim's attachment to Zuleika prevents him from performing his manly duty) as it is a matter of erroneous assumptions about human life that are paid for with life itself.

That Selim is killed and the conspiracy violently crushed does not mean that he is wrong and that Giaffir is right. Giaffir too, it should be remembered, ends distraught, overcome by his daughter's death, and no longer satisfied with his power and position. His despair after the combat connects directly to the social picture in which he figures, projecting the larger implications of his situation. Despite the contradictions pervading Selim's position and despite his adherence to status quo attitudes even when he openly defies ruling authority, his resistance nonetheless points up the inadequacy of the existing order. In the final analysis, Giaffir *is* a tyrant who has risen to power by horrible means, who freely uses his daughter to advance his own political interests, who administers the state without any real regard for public human need. His position exemplifies the inconsistencies pervading the entire social organization he governs and demonstrates why it finally cannot survive. The standard of conduct and action upon which he insists and the superior values he cherishes stem directly from a power structure that overrides and oppresses everything in its way, that denies the fluctuations and intricacies of experience, reducing all life to a flat and fixed definition. Though he is not a sentimental idealist like Selim, he is nonetheless governed by abstract thinking that distorts his view of the world, leading him to believe that absolute control is possible. Like Selim, too, he learns that he cannot "prove all truth" in action despite the fact that the entire social organization is at his disposal; the deeds he sanctions and performs do not place him any closer to absolute power and in fact eventually undermine his power: "The Star hath set that shone on Helle's stream— / What quench'd its ray?—the blood that thou hast shed" (2. 660–61). The issue here is very similar to that which Byron explores in his Napoleon poems. Giaffir fails to realize that all power is circumstantially contained and determined, and eventually he loses touch with the actual conditions that had made his position possible in the first place, so that the very ingredients that had lifted him finally crush him. His demise in some respects is a mirror image of Selim's, traceable directly to the same cause, namely the abstraction of power from its public or even human context.

The Bride tells a story in which nobody wins, neither the passive, the aggressive, the sentimental, the would-be revolutionary, nor the viciously authoritarian. This would seem to suggest that there simply is no way to overcome the pervasive ills troubling human experience. While it is correct to stress this negative element in the poem, it does not follow that failure and doom are absolutely and eternally imbedded in human nature. The narrative events, though they have an abstract and larger-than-life air about them, due largely to the exotic setting and melodramatic descriptions, are rooted in specific human situations, bound up with social and political realities that govern both the attitudes and the actions of the characters. The social conditions that drive Selim into opposition against Giaffir are the same conditions that cause him to idealize Zuleika and that at the same time doom Giaffir to defeat even in victory. Likewise, the beliefs that physical exertion and extension of control are the only positive values in life or, at the other extreme, that the natural landscape can provide a refuge from the violent and arbitrary exertion of power, are traceable directly to the same authoritarian power structure, and constitute not so much right or wrong assessments of reality as manifestations of the various perceptions that are *produced within society.* I do not mean here to reduce social reality to a simple relativist analysis, as though there were no judgments to be made respecting experience. To recognize the physical structures of the world being presented in the poem and their motivating assumptions is to understand what is wrong with that world, to see objectively that it viciously deceives, consumes, and oppresses people, eventually destroying even itself. But it is important to understand that the people involved in these social processes are never independent of them and that they are often blinded or confused by social norms that appear natural, constant, and universal.

While in composing *The Bride* Byron was taking "refuge in Imagination" (*BLJ* 3:185), writing simply "for the sake of the *employment*" (*BLJ* 3:184), generating so much "glitter" (*BLJ* 3:175) for an ignorant public (*BLJ* 3:168), he was also, intentionally or not, addressing the ills, events, and attitudes that virtually had made public involvement impossible for him. He was not even willing (or able) at this time to present a petition in Parliament on behalf of a cause he supported, and for no clear reason. As he remarked at an uncharacteristically vulnerable moment: "I really have not nerves even to present a pet[itio]n far less a word upon it—at this moment—I can't tell why but so it is—either indolence—or hippishness—or incapacity—or all three" (*BLJ* 3:193). The air of defeat and defenselessness here, the very tired voice, and the impression he gives that he simply does not wish to be bothered suggest his need to regroup his intellectual and emotional energies, to regain confidence in the face of events that for more than two years had overwhelmed him. To retreat into poetry was in one way to submit to these events (and as noted above he was embarrassed by this submission), but at the same time it was to find release, to address in his own way, in as loud a voice as he wished, his sense of the sheer chaos surrounding him. Thus, while in public matters he had become apathetic and defeatist, in poetry he was extremely energetic and confident, bubbling with "Oriental names and scenes"

(*BLJ* 3:168). As he remarked to Lord Holland of *The Bride*, "it is my story & my *East*" (*BLJ* 3:168), and he wrote it enthusiastically, scanning freely the range of ideas which captured his imagination. Rejecting the didactic mode as well as a socially responsible poetic voice, he explored and energetically systematized the complex and irreducible concerns of public and private life that otherwise refused to be mastered and that otherwise could be threatening and inhibiting. Written "to dispel reflection during *inaction*" (*BLJ* 3:157), the poem presents an exotic formulation of the powerful forces (obvious and submerged) that contributed to that inaction. Social reality is not absent from the poem but rather is transformed into aesthetically and emotionally manageable terms.

4

The Corsair

BYRON'S letters and journal during the period immediately surrounding the composition of *The Corsair* illustrate clearly that, as McGann puts it, his "weariness and disillusion with Regency society and politics [had] reached a critical level" (*BCPW* 3:445). Not only was he tired of Murray and the Tories (see, for instance, *BLJ* 4:18, 32, and 38); he was frustrated with the Whigs as well, to the extent in fact that he felt tremendous pressure to leave England for good (see *BLJ* 3:217). Characteristically, he responded to his situation by expressing vociferously his contempt for and independence from prevailing opinions. As he told Murray in a letter written within a month after completing *The Corsair*, "my politics are to me like a young mistress to an old man[;] the worse they grow the fonder I become of them" (*BLJ* 4:37). The truth of this statement is evidenced both by his decision to publish his original dedication of *The Corsair* to Thomas Moore, despite Murray's objection that it "was too much about politics" (*BLJ* 4:18), and by his inclusion in the volume (again over Murray's objections) of the inflammatory poem "To a Lady Weeping," which until now he had not acknowledged publicly as his composition, even though the poem had been written in 1812.[1] With respect to the certain public outcry that "the Weepers" (as he called the poem [see *BLJ* 4:80]) would draw upon him, he remarked dismissively, "I care nothing for consequences on this point" (*BLJ* 4: 37). *The Corsair* crystallizes many of the ideas that stand behind the acerbic comments in his letters and journal during this period. By situating the tale between two openly political statements (the dedication and "To a Lady Weeping"), Byron calls attention to its political and intellectual undercurrent and to its importance as a critical response to the disturbing circumstances surrounding him.

While *The Corsair* has its source most immediately in the same personal concerns that had influenced the earlier tales, it is also conditioned in a specific way by Byron's reading of Sismonde de Sismondi during this period, a fact that may have some bearing on the particular tone and direction of the poem. Byron mentions Sismondi twice in his letters and journals shortly after composing *The Corsair* (*BLJ* 3:195, 252) and shows every sign of having known his work well.

McGann, in fact, notes in his commentary on the poem that Byron took Conrad's name from Sismondi, noting as well that Sismondi's "narrative of the history of the defeats of the Ghibelline Party at the end of the thirteenth century is presented as the turning-point in Italian history, when the citizenry began to abandon their adherence to republicanism and to accept the rule of despots" (*BCPW* 3:445).[2] This is an important insight for it suggests a primary focus of *The Corsair*—namely, its effort to depict social life at a moment of extreme crisis, that is, at a moment when important conflicting determinants have intensified to the point where they threaten conventional assumptions about public and private life.

Byron's Conrad probably takes his name from two prominent kings of Germany, Conrad IV and his son, Conrad V. Conrad IV, who succeeded his father, Frederick II, to the throne in 1250, ruled only until 1254, at which time he died suddenly. He spent most of his short tenure as king fighting successfully against the Neapolitan Guelphs in an effort to secure his power over the Two Sicilies, which his father before him had built into a prosperous kingdom. Conrad V came to power in 1267 at the age of sixteen, at which time he attempted to claim the rights of his family, which had been denied by the popes. He was defeated and beheaded, along with many German princes and Ghibelline nobles who had supported him. According to Sismondi, "The defeat and death of Conradin established the preponderance of the Guelph part throughout the peninsula."[3]

These events are important not only because they mark a significant change in the course of Italian history, but also because they call attention to the pervasive social unrest that accompanied the development of merchant culture. In describing events prior to Conrad's defeat, Sismondi speaks of the struggles between the greater and lesser Italian cities in terms of the "commerce and wealth" which increasingly defined public issues, showing his understanding of the historical process by which "the desire of domination succeeded that of independence"[4] in the growing commercial centers. This emphasis on commercialism informs the struggles of Conrad IV and Conrad V and provides a connecting thread for the diverse episodes Sismondi presents. The religious, familial, and political conflicts that were foremost in the history of the period are consistently grounded upon this pervasive issue. Byron incorporates Sismondi's interests into *The Corsair*, using commercialism as the material base for the narrative action, allowing it to direct and encompass every issue. As I shall argue momentarily, the crisis that Byron's Conrad faces emerges directly from the triumph of merchant culture over aristocracy.

In some respects, *The Corsair* follows the earlier tales in its depiction of alienation, individual defiance, and consuming unhappiness, though it presents these more energetically and entertainingly than the previous poems had done. But *The Corsair* is finally different from *The Giaour* and *The Bride* in more ways than it is similar to them, as Byron uses the same general literary format to break new intellectual and aesthetic ground. Not only does he work the Oriental setting more effectively to provide an objective means of examining political and social subjects, but also within this setting he divides his hero from conventional society, not as the Giaour had been divided from Hassan's world, but rather as an open antagonist to its controlling structures. The Giaour's discontent with society had been private, growing largely from his affair with Leila; Conrad's resistance is a way of life that provides the basic goods (food, clothing) and also the general values for an entire clan of people. Further, Byron achieves a degree of social completeness here that had been lacking in the earlier tales by emphasizing the fundamental social role played, for instance, by money and law. The facts that Conrad has no legal right to the wealth Seyd possesses and that his actions attempt to undermine the codes binding society and sanctioning Seyd's authority and wealth indicate powerfully the economic and legal contexts within which the narrative action must be understood. Finally, Byron here introduces two heroines, each with a distinct personality, thus providing a means of developing in greater detail not only the issue of the social role of women but also the question of how abstract thinking controls conduct and perceptions of reality. These and other interests make *The Corsair* a compelling and encompassing articulation of social life, charging the poem with important issues that undergird public conduct and private belief.

The pervasive tendency in studies of *The Corsair* has been to focus attention on Conrad almost to the total exclusion of the world he inhabits. His mysterious allure, his alienation and independence, and his embodiment and projection of the Byronic personality are so powerfully drawn as to appear to be of sole importance in the poem. The story itself, as most readers would have it, is mainly a vehicle used for the display of this enticing and unique character.[5] In fact, however, Conrad is but one actor in a highly complex scheme of events, his decisions, beliefs, and actions but specific instances or components of a larger set of circumstances. A comment by Marx helps to clarify this view of Byron's hero. Speaking theoretically about the individual's relation to the surrounding world, he states that "Man's individual and species-life are not *different*, however much . . . the mode of existence of the individual is a more *particular* or more *general* mode of the life of the species."[6] Or, as Russell Jacoby remarks, "private hopes, desires, and nightmares [are] cued by public and social forces. The social does not 'influence' the private; it dwells within it." This is as true in exotic narrative verse as it is in everyday experience, and with respect to *The Corsair* it means that Conrad's character is, as it were, symptomatic of issues and realities extending well beyond his isolated personality and well beyond his self-conscious projection of himself onto the world. To see only Conrad is to abstract him from his surroundings and thus to distort and to misread his importance. Again to quote Jacoby: "[T]he idea of the individual as an autonomous being . . . [is] ideological."[7] Because Conrad is but one individual within a complex *social* reality, the surest way into the poem is through a critical consideration of the world that has given him his particular life, rather than simply through his own limited perception of that world.

To understand Conrad's world (that is, the world of piracy and plunder) it is necessary to understand first the world he has rejected, because it continues its hold on him, among other ways by supplying him with the material necessities of life. Structurally, this world is not very different from the worlds Selim and the Giaour resisted. Seyd is a coldblooded tyrant wielding absolute power over his subjects without regard for their needs; supported in his position by the accepted religious creed, he understands only two classes of people, rulers and slaves, and the division between them as far as he is concerned is absolute. His power is celebrated and displayed not only through the exercise of violence, which of course is a frequent and sure sign of his right and ability to rule, but also through the elaborate show of wealth, particularly through feasting. Here as elsewhere in his poetry Byron associates eating well with political authority, stressing the banqueting, the "sumptuous fare" (2. 113), even the "salt" (2. 119) and "dainties" (2. 123) that slaves are made to serve up to Seyd and his fellow rulers.

Unlike in the earlier tales, however, Byron here seems particularly aware of the way money serves power and supports political control both physically and ideologically. Seyd's world is shown clearly to be a merchant society, unified and motivated by its function of moving goods and accumulating wealth. While we cannot trace fully the constituent elements of this society, we should observe that Byron would have been particularly sensitive to the merchant issue because the seventeenth and eighteenth centuries constituted what is now recognized as the second great period of merchant development in Western culture, with England of course playing a major role in this development. As Marx explains this historical moment: "Commerce and navigation had expanded more rapidly than manufacture, which played a secondary role; the colonies were becoming considerable consumers; and after long struggles the various nations shared out the opening world market among themselves. The period begins with the Navigation Laws and colonial monopolies. The competition of the nations among themselves was excluded as far as possible by tariffs, prohibitions and treaties; and in the last resort the competitive struggle was carried on and decided by wars (especially naval wars). The mightiest maritime nation, the English, retained preponderance in commerce and manufacture." With the development of a merchant class, Marx states, there arose "the possibility of commercial communications transcending the immediate neighbourhood, a possibility the realisation of which depended on the existing means of communication, the state of public safety in the countryside, which was determined by political conditions (during the whole of the Middle Ages, as is well known, the merchants travelled in armed caravans), and on the cruder or more advanced needs (determined by the stage of culture attained) of the region accessible to intercourse." As this class became socially dominant, literally by "press[ing] for state protection and monopolies," it determined the codes of civilized conduct and thought, creating what Marx calls "the outlook of the big bourgeoisie," that is, an ideology rooted in movable capital and fitted to the conditions that secure and increase monetary gains.[8] It is not surprising, then, under these conditions, which form the unstated but determining elements of the poem's social world, that when Conrad enters Seyd's palace disguised as a Dervise he gains Seyd's ear immediately by explaining that while travelling on a merchant ship "From Scalanova's port to Scio's isle," he was once captured and "the Moslem merchant's gains / The Rovers won" (2. 67–70). Seyd's weakness, as Conrad knows, is his consuming drive to protect movable goods and his zeal to exterminate all threats to these goods.

Merchant wealth informs not only public life, but personal relationships as well. Like William Morris's heroine in "The Defence of Guenevere," Gulnare is "bought" (3. 329) as "a toy for dotard's play" (3. 342). The pervasive importance of money is suggested further by Gulnare's attempt to save Conrad from torture and execution. In pleading Conrad's case before Seyd, she states:

> Methinks, a short release, for ransom told
> With all his treasure, not unwisely sold;
> Report speaks largely of his pirate-hoard—
> Would that of this my Pacha were the Lord!
> While baffled, weakened by this fatal fray—
> Watched—followed—he were then an easier prey;
> But once cut off—the remnant of his band
> Embark their wealth, and seek a safer strand.
>
> (3. 145–52)

When Seyd reproaches her for this speech, she appeals again to the importance of Conrad's wealth: "My thoughts were only to secure for thee / His riches" (3. 165–66). Whereas the worlds of Hassan and Giaffir had been defined mainly by blind power and violence, in Seyd's world these are subsumed by money, which more than any other single concern gives social life its coherence. (This perhaps explains why Seyd comes across as an even more repulsive character than his counterparts in the earlier tales.)

In addition to determining the particular mode of public and personal life, economic relations determine and substantiate the legal structures binding conventional order. Specifically, the tale maintains that legal relations—one of the means by which the State maintains its power—are always controlled and defined by the ruling elite. These relations are not purely quantitative; they are not clearly drawn lines on either side of which stand good and evil or right and wrong: they do not exist only "in the sphere of positive law technically understood," to borrow Gramsci's phrase. They involve the entire network of unstated ideas pervading society and always remain nebulous on some deep level, though they are no less powerful for this. Further, they are flexible, changing as social relations change to serve the demands of the prevailing power structure. According to Gramsci, "through 'law', the State renders the ruling group 'homogeneous', and tends to create a social conformism which is useful to the ruling group's line of development."[9] Or, as Marx puts it, "neither legal relations nor political forms [can] be comprehended . . . by themselves or on the basis of a so-called general development of the human mind, but . . . on the contrary they originate in the material conditions of life."[10] With respect to the narrative, this means that the specific legal structures binding social life are a direct product of the merchant world being portrayed, determined in fundamental ways by economic and class reality. They represent the legitimation of the existing power structure and constitute the socially sanctioned means by which domination is exercised. Thus it is that Conrad, who is described repeatedly (even by himself) as an outlaw, is condemned as a criminal for social rather than for abstract or absolute moral reasons: he is not an outlaw because he is violent, capable of destruction and murder, but because he lives upon "plundered wealth" (2. 78), that is, because his actions challenge the rigid economic relations developed and perpetuated by the powerful merchant class.

Conrad's conscious endorsement and acceptance of outlawry is informed at every point by the involved social relations defining merchant culture. He has been "Warped by the world in Disappointment's school" (1. 253), driven by what he sees as the unjust conditions and principles of a vicious merchant society into adopting an outlaw life that, if finally no better than the world Seyd controls, is at least, he believes, free of the illusions of inherent right and superiority characterizing conventional society:

> He knew himself a villain—but he deemed
> The rest no better than the thing he seemed;
> And scorned the best as hypocrites who hid
> Those deeds the bold spirit plainly did.
>
> (2. 265–68)

From Conrad's point of view, this absence of self-deception requires courage and honesty. While it cannot offer private fulfillment and happiness, it offers a sort of freedom not otherwise available (as the pirates' opening song attests [1. 1–42]) and hence the possibility of moral awareness, loyalty, and strong human commitment.

Whether or not Conrad's understanding of his situation is correct (and I shall suggest momentarily that it is not), his position nonetheless provides an important criticism of the social structures prevailing in his world. His piracy, his open acceptance of villainy and plunder, however disturbing, are a form of social protest that at once exposes the inconsistencies and contradictions of governing social codes, and looks for a way of life that is fundamentally honest. While his protest is largely reactionary and certainly primitive, consisting mainly of isolated attacks on caravans of merchant ships or on militarily superior merchant communities that are both more sophisticated and have greater manpower than Conrad's small clan, still his activities are socially engaged, motivated by the assumption that the new world under the rule of such persons as Seyd is fundamentally vicious and alienating. If his conduct manifests a utopianism that is regressive rather than progressive, values that are primitive rather than modern, social standards that are aristocratic ("Lord" Conrad, he is called) rather than inchoate bourgeois, it nevertheless expresses a vital and compelling need for social fulfillment and social meaning. If he would have a world where public order is certain, where social life is fixed, where values are defined in terms of natural law rather than in terms of money, it is because such a world, he believes, would be more meaningfully human. In short, his banditry, as Marx says generally of crime, "is not the result of pure arbitrariness," even if Conrad believes himself to be acting independently and without discernible motivation, but rather is "the struggle of the isolated individual against predominant relations" that have alienated him. [11]

The issue of banditry is a critical concern in the narrative because it opens the field of social inquiry by providing a negative critique of accepted social conventions. While Peter Thorslev has discussed the literary tradition surrounding this subject with particular emphasis on Byron and the tales, [12] Eric Hobsbawm's writings are more immediately helpful for they focus directly the broad social and historical issues that subsume purely literary historical concerns. According to Hobsbawm, the first truth about banditry historically is that "it is rural, not urban. The peasant societies in which it occurs know rich and poor, powerful and weak, rulers and ruled, but remain profoundly and tenaciously traditional, and pre-capitalist in structure." Banditry is, as it were, "a pre-political phenomenon," [13] though it may become politically conscious under certain conditions. Further, as suggested above, banditry is given cohesiveness by a very conservative, regressive value system. As Hobsbawm puts it, "Insofar as bandits have a 'programme,' it is the defense or restoration of the traditional order of things 'as it should be' (which in traditional societies means as it is believed to have been in some real or mythical past)." [14] While Conrad does not spend much time in the narrative actually lamenting a lost, glorious world, he demonstrates in every action that his beliefs are traditional and that he is desperate to find meaning and hope. He illustrates in his outcry against a rapidly changing world what Raymond Williams (in a different context) has called "the backward look" that characterizes so many writers and thinkers, not to mention fictional characters, of the nineteenth century. [15]

Hobsbawm identifies a variety of bandit types, including peasant bandits, landlord bandits, and state bandits, all of whom share a strong traditionalism. As an aristocrat, Conrad of course is a landlord bandit, and, though he does not fit exactly Hobsbawm's definitions, he displays several important characteristics of his historical type. For instance, he "begins his career of outlawry not by crime, but as the victim of injustice"; he is perceived as a sort of "champion, the righter of wrongs"—at least by the victims of oppression; he is given to "feelings of charity"; he distinguishes between "just or legitimate killing and unjust, unnecessary and wanton murder"; he believes there is a difference between "honourable and shameful acts."[16] This combination of traits sets Conrad apart from the conventions that have come to prevail in his world, isolating him from the social flow of everyday life. Indeed, he appears to be a virtual anachronism, the embodiment of standards and conduct that are all but socially extinct. At the same time, however, these traits enable him to face injustice for, at least on the surface, they represent values that are superior to and are more genuinely compassionate than those defining the system that has outlawed him. His aristocratic temperament, for all its limitations and obvious wrongness, is morally and socially engaged in that it exemplifies the possibility of justice, even in a degraded world. The aristocratic element underpinning his bandit life is a sign of hope and, as we shall see momentarily, an example of honor which encourages resistance to deception and malice.

To recognize Conrad's traditionalism and conservatism is to understand that he is neither blindly defiant and aggressively malicious, nor a pessimist embodying the certainty of universal doom, but rather alienated by a commercial society that denies him the possibility of social awareness and hence of social fulfillment. His hatred of mankind (see, for instance, 1. 403–5) should not be taken as an abstract and absolute denial of all virtue and value, even if Conrad presents it this way, but as a desperate reaction to a world that he believes has become valueless, vicious, and destructive, and that seems to offer no hope of integrity or sense of purpose. That his pronouncements are made with an air of finality and absolute certainty is not so much a sign of his accurate insights into the nature of objective reality as it is a sign of his alienation and lack of awareness, both of which cause him to project his own experiences in universal terms. His actions, for instance his love for Medora, contradict his assertions at every turn, illustrating the specific context in which his comments must be placed to be fully understood.

The traditional values to which Conrad is committed, and which provide the impetus for his powerful resistance, are extremely nebulous and abstract, making them difficult to define. It is possible, however, to sketch certain tendencies within his value system that help to clarify his situation. He defends loyalty in love and in public action, as well as authority grounded upon a notion of public need and community protection—values which he believes are totally incompatible, say, with Seyd's world, where soldiers practice military maneuvers upon their own slaves, where personal relationships are cold, where authority lacks all sense of public responsibility. The vague, desperately noble traditionalism that Conrad opposes to the modern world is exemplified in his attack on Seyd. His first act of siege is to burn Seyd's galleys (which are the primary source of wealth and thus, for him, of all evil), after which he attempts to burn the entire city;

but at the same time he gives strict orders to preserve the women and the helpless:

> Man is our foe, and such 'tis ours to slay:
> But still we spared—must spare the weaker prey.
> Oh! I forgot—but Heaven will not forgive
> If at my word the helpless cease to live.
>
> (2. 205–8)

Displaying true chivalric courage, Conrad and his fellow pirates enter the burning palace, oblivious to pain and danger, to rescue "defenceless beauty" (2. 218), to preserve what are believed to be the only positive attributes of an otherwise corrupt and rightly damned culture. This action displays clearly his old-fashioned belief, to which he is totally committed and for which he would sacrifice his life, that the violence of public, masculine action should never disturb the innocence and serenity of women. Such discrimination makes banditry (for him) more than simply another form of exploitation and oppression and establishes it as a defense and expression of moral earnestness.

The conservatism associated with Conrad's banditry is even more clearly evidenced in the difference between his relationship with Medora and Seyd's relationship with Gulnare, and in fact domestic life here in many ways serves as an embodiment of the larger social conventions and tensions being portrayed. Seyd and Gulnare are not connected by love or affection, or even by any genuine regard for one another; their relationship is grounded entirely upon money, exploitation, and convenience. If Gulnare is a "queen" (2. 224), she is queen only of a group of women collected for Seyd's pleasure. In real human and political terms she is a "slave" (2. 224, 503), devoid completely of will and of public and private rights. Not only is her intervention on behalf of the imprisoned Conrad contemptuously dismissed, exciting Seyd's suspicion that she is plotting against him (3. 177–93); personal concerns respecting her affections and her body are also consistently suppressed under Seyd's domination. Having literally been bought, she is no more than a physical object, valued solely in terms of the return of pleasure for money spent. Just as Conrad is physically chained by Seyd, she is legally bound to him, victimized by money. Economic reality compromises her integrity and her independence of body and mind, and drains her of all human dimension. For her, Seyd's "fondest mood" (2. 264) is simply cold, a sign of his power over every facet of her life. As she tells Conrad:

> He [Seyd] takes the hand I give not—nor withhold,
> Its pulse nor checked—nor quickened—calmly cold:
> And when resigned, it drops a lifeless weight
> From one I never loved enough to hate.
>
> (2. 511–14)

In the face of such blind and absolute power, her only defense is not to think about her situation. Thus, even when Seyd is near her, he is "absent from my thought" (2. 520). Though set amidst exotic surroundings, taking on the appearance of a foreign or fantasy situation, this relationship, at its most fundamental level, is not terribly different from literary relationships drawn specifically to point up the inhumanity of nineteenth-century bourgeois life, for instance the Josiah Bounderby-Louisa Gradgrind affair in *Hard Times*, which is exploitative and economically grounded, resulting ultimately in the literal collapse of the victimized Louisa. In Seyd and Gulnare, Byron convincingly portrays merchant culture, describing its pervasive influence not only on physical and economic relations, but more importantly on the deep structures of everyday life.

The relationship between Conrad and Medora is drawn in diametrically opposite terms, denying economic and even social reality in favor of a more abstract notion of love and affection. This relationship illuminates substantially the social dimension of the narrative. For all his violence and criminality, Conrad is a very conservative lover, entirely monogamous and totally ruled by strict notions of masculine and feminine roles. He is a public man whose daily life is passed among men, not because he enjoys masculine company, nor even because he feels that there is inherent virtue in the company he keeps—in fact, he is constantly despair-ridden—but because his *duty* is to the public sphere. Just as he is committed to public life, even though "He hated man too much to feel remorse" (1. 262), he assigns Medora entirely to the home, where she becomes his "bird of beauty" (1. 346), the embodiment of "unchangeable" love (1. 287), "Unmoved by absence, firm in every clime, / . . . untired by time" (1. 295–96). She is the constant that not only transcends the world to which he is condemned, but that also absorbs the contradictions of that world, thus making it possible for him to endure the daily trials of his life. As he tells Gulnare once he has been imprisoned:

> It is enough—I breathe—and I can bear.
> My sword is shaken from the worthless hand
> That might have better kept so true a brand;
> My bark is sunk or captive—but my love—
> For her in sooth my voice would mount above.
>
> (2. 482–86)

Patiently waiting for him through each of his dangerous excursions, Medora embraces him on his every return, bestowing love upon him, displaying the housed feminine weakness and charm that he supposedly fights to protect. If Conrad defends Medora, however, he cannot succumb to her entirely, for her world is in an important respect unreal, at least in masculine terms. Rather than knowing human action, she knows poetry, "the tale, by Ariosto told, / Of fair

Olympia loved and left of old" (1. 439–40); rather than knowing the victory song that follows battle, she knows love songs that record total devotion and even death for love; rather than knowing the feast of victory, she knows the "Sherbet" and "The grapes' gay juice" (1. 427–28) that accompany sensual pleasure. However alluring these may be, and however central they are to Conrad's love for Medora, they are off limits to him, and for the simple reason that "a worthy chief / May melt, but not betray to woman's grief" (1. 517–18).

Both humanity and inhumanity, domination and hope, are found in this conventional domestic relationship. If the love affair offers to Conrad more than it does to Medora, if it assigns Conrad the dominant role of generating and preserving economic relations while trapping Medora away from the full potential of public life, rendering her powerless and isolated, it still is qualitatively different from the relationship between Seyd and Gulnare. In the mutual exchange of love between Conrad and Medora is contained a vaguely hinted hope that their sincere regard for one another constitutes a domain where two people can express their most serious needs openly and fully, where they come closest to realizing the deep virtue of human contact, where they resist isolation.[17] In this sense, love is a form of opposition to the world Seyd administers. Like banditry, it is a socially significant action, expressing a positive resistance to the values displayed, for instance, in the oppressive relationship between Seyd and Gulnare.

The hopeful social dimension of love relationships is carried into the public sphere when Gulnare becomes attracted to Conrad. The domestic circumstances of Conrad's life display his need for genuine human regard, and indeed the values he finds in the home are one moral impetus for his struggle in the world; that is, his primitive attack on commercialism is on some deep level a defense of personal life as he feels it should be. Thus when he besieges Seyd in a desperate attempt to destroy the conditions that have pushed him into isolation and outlawry, he brings with him values that, even amidst the blood bath he initiates, remain constant, as evidenced by the fact that he interrupts his military exploits to rescue Gulnare and her companions from certain death. As a victim of Seyd's merchant mentality and absolute authority, alienated both sexually and socially, Gulnare is immediately influenced by this humane and generous act. Conrad's gentleness and sincerity, which have been nurtured over time by his love for Medora, represent to her the fulfillment possible in human relationships. In contrast to Seyd's selfishness, "The Corsair vowed protection, soothed affright, / As if his homage were a woman's right" (2. 267–68). He becomes in her eyes a sign of hope, an example of feelings that stand opposed to the brutal and alienating social relations she has known. In short, he awakens her by his kindness to her own humanity and inspires her to struggle for freedom.

If Conrad's behavior defends tradition (or at least a version of tradition), resists a new order of exploitation—in this case, commercialism—and looks back to aristocratic hierarchy and certainty, it nonetheless duplicates and reflects the ruling order in many important ways and is subject finally to the limitations imposed by conventional society. Unable to free himself entirely from the circumstances surrounding him, despite the sincerity and fervor of his protest, and despite his traditionalism, he inevitably takes over many of its unstated assumptions and moves about within parameters established not by himself but by society. Even as an outlaw he is subject to the ideological constraints binding society, and thus there are numerous contradictions between what he sincerely wants and what his actions mean and do, though these contradictions are consistently elided by the abstract values governing his thought.

The ideological dimensions of bandit life become apparent immediately in certain elements of Conrad's character, and in the belief among the outlaws that Conrad somehow embodies special, superhuman powers. He is described early in the narrative as unique and inscrutable, as the embodiment of characteristics superior to ordinary human manners, and thus as the rightful possessor of absolute authority:

> And who dare question aught that he decides?
> That man of loneliness and mystery,
> Scarce seen to smile, and seldom heard to sigh;
> Whose name appals the fiercest of his crew,
> And tints each swarthy cheek with sallower hue;
> Still sways their souls with the commanding art
> That dazzles, leads, yet chills the vulgar heart.
> What is that spell, that thus his lawless train
> Confess and envy, yet oppose in vain?
> What should it be? that thus their faith can bind?
> The power of Thought—the magic of the Mind!
>
> (1. 172–83)

This description makes Conrad appear to be free of all social determinations, to exist, in Promethean fashion, as the embodiment of pure mind, independent of the demands that subdue lesser men. His independence and power, supposedly, develop magically out of a soul that is deeper than other souls. In fact, however, Conrad is thoroughly imbued with culture; he is striking not because he is free of all determinations, but—precisely the reverse—because so many determinations combine to form his character. Specifically, his situation graphically illustrates David Erdman's remark that Byron's heroes "often appear acutely conscious of the mortality of their own class."[18] As a noble outlaw he is faced directly with the inevitable triumph of merchant culture, and the crisis that his social class faces is everywhere apparent in his character.

His mysteriousness results largely from this "absent cause" in the narrative, which fully mediates his personality. As Fredric Jameson puts it (writing in a different context), there are "alienating necessities"[19] (i.e., the unavoidable pressures of historical reality) that, however much we ignore them or suppress them, produce reality as we know it and experience it, and that in *The Corsair* are wholly responsible for Conrad's ostensibly abstract personality. Literally stated, Conrad's apparent freedom from and superiority to both Seyd and to his own followers in fact is a response to fragmentation and alienation originating in actual social conditions. His position and personality are "dictated by the economic social structure of society," by the exigencies of the merchant culture which prevails. In social terms he is not free; he is lost. He is not superior; he is isolated. The magic and mystery of his character do not illustrate his independence (though they appear to) but, quite the reverse, suggest the extremity of his alienation in the face of the economic and ideological frameworks governing his life. What is passed off as private strength is finally no more than extreme rejection by a culture that has destroyed aristocratic hegemony. His survival and leadership do not depend on his ability to overcome alienation, but rather on his ability to transcend it "by universalizing it," that is, by denying class reality and by insisting on the inherent value of the very characteristics that mark his frustration. He is an example, in short, of what Russell Jacoby calls "the gloss of freedom under the conditions of its denial."[20]

This view suggests that, even while he protests, and even while he cultivates his heroic stature, Conrad remains wholly attached to and governed by the codes of conventional society. The extent to which this is true is readily seen in his exercise of power, which is largely an obverse duplication of Seyd's position. His authority is no less absolute and rigid than the authority he rejects; no less than Seyd, he denies inquiry into his motives: "And all obey and few enquire his will; / To such, brief answer and contemptuous eye / Convey reproof, nor further deign reply" (1. 80–82). Further, he maintains his position not so much by his physical bravery and skill as by his uncomplaining acceptance of what is unanimously believed to be the burden of power:

> The many still labour for the one!
> 'Tis Nature's doom—but let the wretch who toils
> Accuse not, hate not *him* who wears the spoils.
> Oh! if he knew the weight of splendid chains,
> How light the balance of his humbler pains.
>
> (1. 188–92)

His authority exploits generally held beliefs about leadership, cultivating awe and admiration among his followers so that they do not challenge his right to govern. His power is secure because his followers believe that his position is worse than theirs. He is allowed to direct their labors to his benefit because they believe that they are better off laboring for him than for themselves. He enjoys absolute political control because everyone believes that power *naturally* gravitates to one person, a belief of course reinforced by the commercial world suffering under Seyd's tyrannical authority. Given the choice between Seyd and Conrad, the latter appears to the pirates more humane, more sincere, more virtuous, more clearly committed to freedom and bravery.

Approached in terms of these ideological assumptions, Conrad's mysteriousness dissolves, and he is shown to occupy a station that has been socially defined, to condemn Seyd while at the same time clinging tenaciously to a political structure that distributes power in an identical fashion. No less than his enemy, he is an exploiter of people, relying on common assumptions about social reality to maintain his authoritarian control. This is not to condemn his resistance to an obviously villainous culture, but to emphasize, as suggested earlier, that he does not magically rise above it, nor stand abstractly in opposition to it. To perceive him as fundamentally separate from the world he rejects, as uniquely unsuited to life among merchants, is to accept uncritically the ideological formulations defining that world, to accept that individuals can free themselves from social reality, if they are only strong enough to do so. For all his detachment, he is finally a participant in and a material beneficiary of a system constructed along definite economic, political, and class lines. He works this system to his advantage (unconsciously, to be sure) by perpetuating social and political ignorance and alienation, by nurturing the belief that individual power is natural and that it naturally though mysteriously falls to him.

An additional indication of the extent to which Conrad remains within the conventions of his world is his attitude towards physical violence. It is true that he excepts women and the helpless from his acts of villainy, but otherwise he plunders the countryside mercilessly, so much so that a detached observer might have difficulty distinguishing his exploits from Seyd's. Fearless of death, and with only momentary lapses of softness of heart, Conrad lives by ambush, accepting unquestioningly bloodshed and murder carried out by the most vicious means imaginable (note, for instance, his exploitation of religion to penetrate an enemy camp). While the pirates await their secret attack on Seyd, "their leader [leaned] o'er the fretting flood, / And calmly talked—and yet he talked of blood" (1. 605–6). He is presented repeatedly as an inspirer of terror who does not blink at even the worst violence:

> He saw their terror. . . .
>
> . . . .
> Completes his fury, what their fear begun,
> And makes the many basely quail to one.
> The cloven turbans o'er the chamber spread,
> And scarce an arm dare rise to guard its head:
> Even Seyd, convulsed, o'erwhelm'd, with rage, surprize,
> Retreats before him, though he still defies.
>
> . . . .
> . . . . the din
> Of groaning victims, and wild cries for life,
> Proclaimed how well he did the work of strife.
>
> (2. 165, 172–77, 187–89)

Doubtless Conrad perceives his attack on Seyd as an honorable act, as an effort to exterminate true villainy, but the slaughter, and more significantly the zealous enactment of violence, undermine his credibility and raise serious questions about the value he places on human life. That violence and slaughter are unquestioned practices, that they are beyond dispute and examination, is suggested by his response to his eventual capture. Not only does he see his imminent execution as "right" (2. 443) because his attack failed; he confesses as well that violent strength is the source of value for him: "Unfit to vanquish— shall I meanly fly, / The one of all my band that would not die" (2. 472–73)? From his perspective, failure in battle deserves punishment by torture and death. However much his actions result from and conversely expose social ills, they do not achieve full independence from these ills, but in fact unfold along a common ground of value and interpretation.

Another way Conrad betrays his submission to the deep structure governing social life is through his perception of and conduct towards women. As suggested above, his love for Medora constitutes a hope that is not present in the relationship between Seyd and Gulnare; it illustrates the human need for sexual and social fulfillment. At the same time, however, the specific enactment of this love shares important characteristics with prevailing social codes, particularly in its subjection of Medora. Seyd of course literally and willfully dominates Gulnare, subjecting her by means of economic and political superiority to his sexual gratification, so that injustice is obvious. Because the relationship between Conrad and Medora is grounded upon a concept of love rather than expressly upon money, injustice is more difficult to perceive or to imagine, though it is no less real. In fact, the bottom line of their relationship, too, is money, though neither of them realizes this. Medora takes no part whatsoever in the social production or acquisition of the necessities of life—indeed, she is denied any such role by Conrad—and thus becomes physically and emotionally isolated, increasingly dependent on Conrad's public life for her physical and emotional sustenance. If their relationship is a sign of real human need, its specific dimensions project once more the alienating culture in which they participate. Medora becomes a possession, a commodity, a private repository of emotional resources. Conrad perceives not only Medora but all women in this light, as evidenced by his daring rescue of the women in Seyd's harem. Although his attitude is perhaps preferable to Seyd's, it is not finally a liberating position, but is in fact an extension of the class values and patriarchal assumptions that originate in the world Seyd inhabits and that Conrad believes he has rejected.

This issue illustrates compellingly the facts that in substantial ways Conrad and Seyd occupy the same world and that this world is torn by severe contradictions. As in *The Giaour* and *The Bride*, Byron here focuses on the idealization of women, elevating it to a position of vital social importance and thereby suggesting once again the necessity of radically reassessing human relationships.[21] Not only is Medora presented in one-dimensional and abstract terms, as a "bird of beauty," as Conrad's only hope in life (1. 400); more importantly, Gulnare is portrayed in the same way, at least initially. When she visits Conrad in prison she is described as a "heavenly face" (2. 397), as a "form" (2. 402), as a "shape of fairy lightness—naked foot, / That shines like snow, and falls on earth as mute" (2. 404–5)—in short, she fully embodies the "defenceless beauty" that Conrad had risked his life to preserve. This attitude is entirely in line with the thinking of protagonists in the earlier tales and illustrates Conrad's utopian impulse, his desire for values that somehow are cleansed of the inconsistencies in every day life that have alienated him.

The problem of course is that Conrad's thinking is directly challenged in a way that earlier heroes' attitudes had not been. It is true that in *The Giaour* and *The Bride* the idealized heroines die, proving their own vulnerability and the consequent inadequacy of their lovers' perceptions of the world. But in neither poem is the hero forced to confront directly the implications of his thought. In *The Bride* Selim dies before Zuleika and thus is freed from having to face life without her; and in *The Giaour*, even though Leila dies, she remains idealized through the Giaour's memory of her—in fact, her significance as an abstract ideal increases rather than diminishes after her death, as the Giaour, in the monastery, recreates her along religious lines.

Not only does Gulnare not die; she refuses to submit passively to the social controls that make women the objects rather than the subjects of human experience. Inspired to action by Conrad's valiant rescue of her, she feels sufficiently strong to resist the power Seyd had exercised over her, to become herself a criminal committed to making Seyd "bleed" (3. 319). Her intentions, however, overwhelm Conrad, who is not a revolutionary but a pirate, not a political challenger to the external and internal structures of society but an alienated man who yet clings to the codes that have alienated him: "Thine [life] saved I gladly, Lady, not for this" (3. 366). His rescue of Gulnare was never intended to have political and social ramifications, but was meant as a deed of devotion to the purity and helplessness of the weaker sex; it was never meant to provide an inspiration for the overthrow of conventional and presumably natural relations between men and women, but to preserve them. Faced with the prospect of Gulnare murdering Seyd, Conrad is incapacitated, his most basic assumptions shaken to their foundations.

Gulnare's activism constitutes an unprecedented reversal in the tales, developing the gender (and hence social) issue further than before. Here, rather than Conrad rescuing Gulnare, *she rescues him*. While Conrad remains isolated in his cell, literally enchained, she enters the public world of action and physical violence, fighting to defend the man she loves. Her attitude towards him is akin to his previously unexamined attitude towards women; he becomes, in her eyes, an ideal—"What sudden spell hath made this man so dear?" (2. 424)—and her objective is to preserve this ideal from "the oppressor Seyd" (3. 357). Without pressing this matter too far, we might observe that this reversal displays literally what before had been ideological: Conrad's cell, from this view, parallels the

home in which Medora dwells; Gulnare's surreptitious attack on Seyd parallels
Conrad's own ambush of Seyd. Such a reversal places Conrad squarely in a
feminine position; he is rendered powerless to determine his own fate, powerless
even to decide what is best for him. Just as he earlier had ignored Medora's plea
that he stay home, Gulnare ignores his plea that she not assassinate Seyd,
dismissing murder as "but a blow" (3. 375). From the moment Gulnare commits
murder to rescue him, he is in her power, the object of rather than the
participant in action, completely stripped of the masculine assumptions and
qualities that heretofore had made him independent and given him courage in
both life and death:

> He had seen battle—he had brooded lone
> O'er promised pangs to sentenced guilt foreshown;
> He had been tempted—chasten'd—and the chain
> Yet on his arms might ever there remain:
> But ne'er from strife—captivity—remorse—
> From all his feelings in their inmost force—
> So thrilled—so shuddered every creeping vein,
> As now they froze before that purple stain.
> That spot of blood, that light but guilty streak,
> Had banished all the beauty from her cheek!
> Blood he had viewed—could view unmoved—but then
> It flowed in combat, or was shed by men!
>
> (3. 418–29)

Faced with truly progressive action, that is, with action that challenges basic
social formulations, he is shattered. Freed by Gulnare's bloody hand, he immediately becomes an emotional prisoner, emptied of courage and sense of purpose,
now helpless to translate his alienation into defiance and struggle: ". . . on his
heavy heart such sadness sate, / As if they there transferred that iron weight [his
chains]" (3. 442–43). As he escapes with Gulnare he is transformed from
protector to protected, from master to subject, from a powerful and mysterious
leader identified by an indomitable will to a meek and confused follower:
". . . Conrad following, at her beck, obeyed, / Nor cared he now if rescued or
betrayed" (3. 448–49).

Several additional touches elaborate the social significance of this episode.
Conrad remains convinced even after his escape that Gulnare has compromised
herself entirely, both in the eyes of the world and in the eyes of heaven. For a
woman to commit murder, he believes, is for her to commit an absolute and
unforgivable sin. Yet he understands as well that he is implicated directly in her
crime and that he cannot escape its hold on him. When he embraces her, fragile
and exhausted after her deed, he acknowledges her and commits himself to her;
that is, he accepts the truly criminal and outcast domain into which he has
unwillingly yet inevitably entered.

This scene is followed immediately by an equally important event, Medora's death. On the level of allegory, she must die because her validity as an ideal and the hope she represents have been destroyed. The course of events has denied her the ability to provide any longer the conventional domestic warmth that she previously had embodied; she can no longer serve as a repository of emotional life capable of absorbing the contradictions and relieving the tensions pervading the public world to which Conrad is condemned. She passes from the scene as Gulnare ascends to dominance, bringing a new, fearful, and admittedly questionable set of values into the world that Conrad had once confidently con-'trolled.

These two moments—the embrace of Conrad and Gulnare, the death of Medora—are the culminating events in the series that has taken Conrad ever further from the traditional values he desperately wanted to preserve. From the instant of Medora's death, he is alone with Gulnare, for better or worse, having entered upon a new experience that is qualitatively different from (and yet as undefinable as) the fundamentally hopeful life he had previously led.[22]

These closing scenes illustrate graphically the extent to which history resists desire.[23] The depth of Conrad's conservatism is everywhere evident, and yet this is powerfully overcome by circumstance and necessity. From the beginning he chisels away at the powers controlling merchant society, motivated by a deep commitment to an older (if mythical) way of life. But at every turn he also unknowingly embraces, as we have seen, certain values vitally attached to the world he has rejected. Because he is a part of the totality of social life, shaped by both its old and new assumptions, he cannot see society as it is in its full complexity; he cannot remove himself from mediating forces sufficiently to understand even the degree to which his own thoughts and actions respond to and change the course of human experience. Thus, despite his traditionalism and despite the ostensibly private character and motivation of his conduct, he perforce helps to create the basis for substantive, progressive, and encompassing change. Because he possesses at best only a partial awareness of social life, and because circumstances create him as much as he creates circumstance, he is drawn inevitably into a position that provides the physical, emotional, and moral impulse for the levelling of existing codes, even to the bedrock level. That he is repulsed and incapacitated by the culminating and inevitable consequence of his exploits clearly illustrates his lack of social understanding and emphatically portrays the discrepancy between his assumption that his actions are personally motivated and traditionally inclined and the reality that these actions constitute public interventions.

This is not to suggest that Conrad's piracy culminates in the overthrow of merchant society, that the encompassing and constraining codes of commercial culture dissolve after Gulnare murders Seyd. Rather, it is to suggest that continued and powerful resistance to prevailing structures—even if that resistance is vitally connected to prevailing ideological controls, as Conrad's resistance is—

begins eventually to challenge accepted values and to uncover new possibilities and directions for social life. The pressure that Conrad exerts on the world under Seyd's power exposes the contradictions of that world (and at the same time of his own world) and thus makes plain the need for substantive change. His kindness towards Gulnare, for instance, makes her aware that she cannot be both queen and slave at once and that in real terms she is only a slave. If his actions are never consciously political, they have political potential simply by virtue of their resistance to prevailing social codes. This point is evidenced in Gulnare's confession that she plans to assassinate Seyd. Having gained entry into Conrad's cell by winning the confidence of a guard who is "Ripe for revolt" (3. 313), she tells Conrad:

> That hated tyrant [Seyd], Conrad—he must bleed!
> I see thee shudder—but my soul is changed—
> Wronged—spurned—reviled—and it shall be avenged—
> Accused of what till now my heart disdained—
> Too faithful, though to bitter bondage chained.
> Yes, smile!—but he had little cause to sneer,
> I was not treacherous then—nor thou too dear:
> But he has said it—and the jealous well,
> Those tyrants, teasing, tempting to rebel,
> Deserve the fate their fretting lips foretell.
>
> (3. 319–28)

Even against his will Conrad is part of an ongoing social process involving at once the powers of legitimation and resistance, convention and change. Although he understands his outlawry in largely personal terms, his intervention contributes substantially (to his regret) to the politicization of social life, to such an extent, in fact, that he undermines his own most cherished assumptions about traditional values and destroys his own future—he is drawn unhappily into "the experience of Necessity,"[24] into a world that emphatically denies his abstractions and ideals.

The poem's ambiguous conclusion suggests the complexity of the subject matter. The narrative creates a social world pervaded by obvious and submerged (suppressed) contradictions, and it confronts these contradictions vigorously and energetically. Further, it convincingly shows the social dimension of all individual experience and the extent to which particular events are subject to the contradictions inherent in certain social circumstances. And yet for all this Byron never approaches a resolution. If anything, he moves further away from certainty and conviction here than in earlier poems. When Conrad and Gulnare disappear from both social worlds at the end of the narrative, leaving the merchants and the pirates to continue struggling as they might, they begin a new life together, so Byron implies (though even this is unclear), of *pure* criminality. That is, their actions have led to an explosion of conventional norms that leaves them permanently outside the realm of ordinary social expectation and responsibility. Like Mary Shelley's Monster at the conclusion of *Frankenstein*, they disappear into a swirl of ambiguities, confident only that problems have been exposed and that solutions are not readily available.

At the same time, however, the conclusion is not exactly pessimistic—it is, again, ambiguous. After all, the action does accurately identify discrepancies within the fabric of social existence. Conrad and Gulnare, criminals as they are, exit from the story inextricably bound to one another in a way that had been impossible in other relationships described in the poem. While the earlier relationships had been grounded upon domination, theirs moves toward equality. After her awful crime, Gulnare is "woman still" (3. 522); and Conrad, while shattered, is not known to have succumbed to his grief. While they do not experience the kind of love that Conrad had felt for Medora, neither do they experience the contradictions of that love. The narrative proceeds relentlessly in its social analysis, never succumbing to an easy or pat solution to obvious difficulties. In the very process of disclosing social hardship, the poem strikes a positive note—the undermining of conventional understanding contains the possibility of reconstruction.

5

Lara

D URING the months between the publication of *The Corsair* (February 1814) and the composition of *Lara* (May 1814) Byron's frustration with Regency politics was heightened by events on the international scene, which drove him virtually to distraction. From mid-February 1814 he knew that Napoleon's days were numbered, though he continued to hope that the French general somehow would survive (*BLJ* 3:243), and he knew as well that his own political and intellectual perspectives were inextricably bound to Napoleon's fate. Although he was by no means an uncritical supporter of Napoleon, he believed that any hope for substantive political improvement in England and Europe depended largely upon Napoleon's success. The removal of Napoleon from the political scene, he believed, would be devastating, for it inevitably would usher in an age of extremely powerful conservatism—politically and ideologically—effectively halting what until now he had thought was the flow of history towards freedom (see, for instance, *BLJ* 3:218). Even if his own frequent calls for the establishment of a republic noticeably lacked deep conviction and confidence, and even if he could offer no specific ideas about how society might be or should be restructured, he looked forward to Napoleon's defeat with dread and even with bitterness.

Written under the pressure of these developments, *Lara* projects Byron's strong fear of returning to a "dull, stupid old system" (*BLJ* 3:218) of absolute rule. The poem's importance to Byron's thinking, however, is obscured by its expository method. Karl Kroeber, for example, whose insights into the social themes in all of Byron's tales are quite helpful, complains of *Lara* that "the indefiniteness of time and locale weakens what might have been a powerful narrative."[1] In fact, however, the poem's indefiniteness stands at the very center of its social interest. That time and place, as well as actions and sentiments, are shrouded in mystery is disturbing because it reflects the extent to which social processes have become mystified, not because it offers a world devoid of historical content. Byron seems to have worked consciously to create the dark, oppressive quality that characterizes the narrative, for he studiously avoided specific details and adamantly refused to provide the vaguest hint of a context for the story. As he remarked to Murray, responding to the various public efforts to situate the poem: ". . . the name only is Spanish—the country is not Spain but the Moon" (*BLJ* 4:146). Further, he knowingly confused the social terminology in the poem, remarking for instance in a note that his use of the term "serf" was largely fortuitous, and that in reality it "could not be correctly applied to the lower classes in Spain, who were never vassals of the soil" (*BCPW* 3:453). This strategy of obscuring the contextual dimensions of the narrative focuses the need to look to the deeper structures of ideas in the tale that can explain confusion and mystery as symptomatic rather than as constitutive. At this level, the tale is remarkably consistent in exposition and powerfully engaged in social inquiry, offering a credible, semi-systematic account of a world in extreme turmoil, a world that constantly misperceives events. The indefiniteness that Kroeber complains of is in this view a sign of what troubles this world; it is a projection of the apparently invisible though certainly oppressive conditions that pervade the entire culture being portrayed in the poem.

We can glimpse the broad social concerns in *Lara* most readily by considering the tale in the light of its predecessor, *The Corsair*. The most striking and important difference between these tales is that in *Lara* Byron avoids any reference whatsoever to the commercial world that had been central in the earlier tale, turning his attention instead to an older aristocratic culture. This radical shift of focus represents more than a reactionary impulse against commercialism and more than a utopian longing for an ideal past, although these obviously inform the narrative in important ways. It provides a full exposition of the conflict and struggle at the center of a social landscape that is often narrowly perceived as static and unthreatened by the march of history, and specifically unthreatened by economics and class struggle. As McGann rightly notes, the uncompromising portrayal of feudal life in *Lara* gives "an implicit explanation of why he [Lara] left in the first place, and why he took up his career as a Noble Outlaw."[2] This point is important because it recognizes that the concept of the Noble Outlaw is not a given, but is in fact a manifestation of specific social relations. In directing our attention to this social context, McGann enables us to see more clearly how the poem builds upon ideas that had been introduced in *The Corsair*. While *The Corsair* had presented a compelling criticism of merchant life, the tale had failed to examine the conditions out of which commercialism had grown, and in fact had presented a hero, Conrad, who assumed unquestioningly that precommercial society was inherently good. What such a society actually would have been like is never suggested in the tale, its quality and substance suppressed by ideological assumptions of past greatness and integrity.

As an imaginative projection of the social relations that would have prevailed under feudalism, *Lara* challenges these assumptions and denies the inherent virtue of aristocratic structures of authority. Feudal society, however much it is supported by a tradition of aristocracy and hierarchical order, never approaches the integrity which Conrad had imagined and which Lara desires because it is not transparent; that is, it does not consist entirely of Lara's sense of what it should be and does not yield readily to his authority. This means that he must contend not simply with his own perception of events, but also with the material conditions encompassing and defining these perceptions. Although he dislikes any reference to the context of his life, he is constantly confronted with questions about his past. He must live daily not only with unhappy relatives, but also with laborers who whisper behind his back (1. 131–54) and with fellow aristocrats who suspect his integrity, making his rank, his power, and, more broadly, even feudal life itself a terrible burden for him. Rather than matching his dreams of what social life might be, the world he inhabits is powerfully governed by actual social relations, effectively shattering the idealization of feudal society that in *The Corsair* had absorbed and sustained the alienated Conrad.

The social relations and conditions under feudalism that bear most directly on *Lara* can be sketched very briefly. Two main points are commonplace, but still need to be mentioned because Byron draws heavily on them. First, feudal society was rigidly divided along class lines, with landlords and tenants forming the major classes. (Above these classes, of course, and sometimes in conflict with both, stood the king, in whom all power ultimately rested, at least theoretically.) Class division was maintained by various means, initially by sheer physical force, and later by the institution of serfdom, which legitimized the authority of the landlords. Second, feudal society was almost wholly agrarian, its labor force based on the family unit and its economy structured along essentially nonmarket lines, that is, along lines determined by factors other than supply and demand. As one historian explains this dimension of feudal society: ". . . peasants produced mainly for their own consumption and rarely exchanged commodities. . . , [while] the feudal lord likewise rarely resorted to trade for almost everything he needed was produced by serf labor."[3]

While these economic and class divisions strengthened the ruling order in feudal society by subordinating questions of domination and social justice to the compelling and more immediate requisites of the land, they also provided the basis for the far-reaching crisis that helped to destroy feudalism. It is true that under the feudal system serfs were directly chained to property, with little or no control over the social means of production; as serfs, laborers served estates rather than themselves alone, and the surplus goods they produced were appropriated by landowners. At the same time, however, they possessed a relative independence as farmers that laborers of earlier and later cultures did not, and this enabled them to become a significant political voice, which eventually challenged the prevailing structures of feudal society. As R. H. Hilton puts it: "Peasants, in their communities and as controllers of the self-contained family were not *economically* dependent on lords. For this reason their potentialities for resistance were not negligible. Hence, if the levy of rent was determined not so much by market forces as by the relative strength of the antagonists, a strengthening of peasant resistance reduced the level of rent transferred to the ruling class—and of tax to the state. This was one of the roots of the crisis of the feudal order."[4]

Over and above the fundamental economic structures of society, order was maintained by various means, including such ideological constraints as jurisdiction. On this subject, A. L. Morton has pointed out that "with the advent of powerful semi-feudal lords the authority of the traditional courts was weakened, and they were supplemented and in part superseded by the granting to these same lords of the right to hold courts of their own," which in turn enabled them "to levy taxes and to exact services."[5] The advantage that the complex legal system in feudal society had over brute force was that its authority was deeply enmeshed within the pervasive systems of value and belief that underpinned feudalism and was sustained by the consent of those over whom it was exercised.[6] In explaining the far-reaching power of jurisdiction, Hilton describes its direct connection to the spiritual and religious assumptions found within feudal culture: ". . . [T]he [legal] assemblies were based on a tripartite division of society, between the church, the nobility and the 'third estate' (the towns). This reflected the ideological vision of the divinely created society of orders, divided between those who prayed (the clergy), those who fought (the nobility) and those who worked (peasants). In this organic view of society the orders of the body politic were mutually supportive and had defined roles outside which no one born or appointed to a particular order (or estate) must step. To do so would not only be a crime against the social order but a sin against God."[7]

Additional ideological features of feudalism are suggested most clearly by the poem itself, which develops fairly extensively the values and attitudes that reflected, shaped, and gave coherence to feudal culture. The celebrations, parties for the elite, and displays of military prowess that abound in the narrative project much more than simply the glitter and gore of an exotic world from the past. These are the most immediate and obvious manifestations of an embracing system of beliefs, ranging from the commonly held assumption that inherited power is natural, absolute, and right, to the belief that honor is abstract and unyielding, that virtue requires the explicit support of existing norms, that land ownership is sacred—in short, that aristocracy and aristocratic values define the limits of social reality.

These social relations and conditions dominate the world of the poem, wielding hegemonic power over every facet of the feudal culture being described. While there are voices of dissent (for instance, "the impatient heir" [1. 37], and even the unhappy Lara himself), the *social* response to the existing order is positive and supportive of governing codes. Even the insurrection that eventually erupts cannot be considered a substantial negative critique of feudalism, for it arises from a matter of principle and honor rather than from a politically conscious assessment of events. Violent and intense as the military skirmish is, it never materially challenges either the prevailing conditions or the attitudes that undergird culture. For instance, even while Lara's supporters condemn tyranny and oppression, they do not denounce aristocratic leadership, following Lara willingly in his personal quarrel with Otho. And while Lara expressly denies common cause with his fellow aristocrats, even fighting to the death with Otho, he never actually relinquishes the authority or the privilege of his aristocratic position, nor veers radically from ruling-class principles. The voices of resistance and the expressions of despair remain largely isolated and private (despite their frequency), while the dominant beliefs that bind society and form the way of life presented in the narrative remain firm and, for the most part, go untested. As Byron presents it, feudal values reach deep into the heart of society, their pervasive presence (developed and strengthened through the long, slow processes of history) subsuming the various contradictions and inconsistencies which emerge through the narrative.

While the narrative establishes the encompassing power of social relations, at the same time it insists upon the difficulty of seeing these relations clearly, and in fact it suggests that events often appear to take place arbitrarily, independently of any social imperative. The mystery of social relations, in fact, is an abiding issue in the tale, and the various actions, characterizations, and perspectives that make up the narrative provide glosses on this mystery.

One of the most obvious instances of this is the depiction of the past, particularly the depiction of Lara's personal history. In many ways, Lara is a superb example of Lukàc's definition of the hero in modern literature. He is "conceived . . . [as] an ahistorical being," injected into the story "without personal history. . . . He does not develop through contact with the world; he neither forms nor is formed by it." Thus he seems to be the embodiment of "the human condition: Man is now what he has always been and always will be."[8] His characterization, abstract and overpowering as it is, does not, however, go unexamined in the narrative, but, on the contrary, becomes a major focus for social inquiry, the mystery of his past revealing the extent to which an entire culture has lost the ability to think historically. At one point it is noted of Lara that:

> Not much he lov'd long question of the past,
> Nor told of wondrous wilds, and desarts vast
> In those far lands where he had wandered lone,
> And—as himself would have it seem—unknown.
>
> (1. 85–88)

In one respect these lines recall Conrad and the Giaour—Lara believes that his past is no one's business but his own, that it is irrelevant to the position he presently occupies in society. Unlike in the earlier narratives, however, the question of personal history is developed into a central issue. While it is presented initially as a private matter, Lara's past becomes much more than gossip and much more than the subject of an isolated quarrel between himself and Ezzelin—as the focal point of the narrative action, it achieves a symbolic function. Touching at some point or another every character in the story, Lara's specific situation calls the entire social world of the poem into life. His personal encounter with Ezzelin gives way to a less personal encounter with Otho, which in turn modulates into a violent military battle between whole armies, throwing the entire culture into momentary turmoil. In terms of these larger events, his past (however narrowly or privately he understands it himself) is socially significant, and caught up in its mystery is the complicated network of relations governing his world.

The most striking fact about Lara's past of course is that no one understands it, though everyone tries. It is, as it were, a point of interest that shows ignorance giving way to confusion and then eventually to violence. Every action in the story that might yield substantial knowledge about Lara is somehow deflected so that his situation becomes ever more obscure, in direct proportion to the growing public interest in him. At the very most, we learn in the conclusion of the story that Lara's body is scarred and that he was thus probably engaged in past violent conflicts of one sort or another. Beyond this, all we are told is that he was once energetically ambitious and that at some point ambition gave way to disillusion and alienation:

> 'Twas strange—in youth all action and all life,
> Burning for pleasure, not averse from strife;
> Woman—the field—the ocean—all that gave
> Promise of gladness, peril of a grave,
> In turn he tried—he ransack'd all below,
> And found his recompence in joy or woe,
> No tame, trite medium; for his feelings sought
> In that intenseness an escape from thought:
> The tempest of his heart in scorn had gazed
> On that the feebler elements hath rais'd;
> The rapture of his heart had look'd on high,
> And ask'd if greater dwelt beyond the sky:
> Chain'd to excess, the slave of each extreme,
> How woke he from the wildness of that dream?
> Alas, he told not!—but he did awake
> To curse the wither'd heart that would not break.
>
> (1. 115–30)

Such information explains very little, despite the curiosity it arouses, and this fact is important to the narrative action. The central plot issue in the tale, Lara's obscure past is a source of personal and social confusion, focusing the inability of characters to gain full knowledge of a subject that they consider to be of vital public significance. In this respect, the narrative gives itself to us in terms of what the culture being described does not know, and this fact should warn us not to accept at face value the self-representations offered in the story. To understand fully the poem's social dimension, we must look beyond these self-representations and explain the *sources* and *context* of the confusion and half-knowledge that characterize Lara's world.

Byron elaborates the importance of the past in the narrative by focusing on the social and historical dimension of language. At least since late 1813 he had been intrigued by the nature of language, raising a compelling question in his journal: ". . . and are not '*words things?*' and such '*words*' very pestilent '*things*' too?" (*BLJ* 3:207). That this question was of crucial and abiding importance to him is suggested by the fact that it remained with him through his entire life. As he wrote years later in *Don Juan:* "But words are things, and a small drop of ink, / Falling like dew, upon a thought, produces / That which makes thousands, perhaps millions, think" (3. 88). In *Lara* he seems concerned to assert not so much that words are things, but rather that, as things, they are terribly pestilent, particularly in their relation to our knowledge of human experience. He makes this point by bringing Lara several times to the verge of confession, only to have him begin to speak "In terms that seem not of his native tongue" (1. 230), so that full knowledge of his life is impossible to achieve. At the beginning of the narrative, when he falls mysteriously into a convulsion, and again near the conclusion, just before he dies, Lara makes apparently critical statements about his situation; and yet his comments are never allowed into the story because, as it is bluntly stated, "They were not such as Lara should avow, / Nor he [Kaled] interpret" (1. 238–39).

This peculiar emphasis on Lara's command of a foreign language, which he falls back on to express his most important ideas, serves at the plot level to heighten his exotic personality and to increase public curiosity about his past. But the point here is not simply that his untranslated speeches contain information that might explain his situation in an individualist or biographical manner (though the narrative states explicitly that they do contain such information; see, for instance, 2. 444–53). More important is the way they symbolize the limiting patterns of thought governing the world of the poem: these speeches constitute the point beyond which feudal culture cannot get in its attempt to understand the past.

Searching for hard evidence that will condemn Lara, society *assumes* the existence of information (apparently contained in Lara's foreign language speeches) that can be appropriated directly and known absolutely and that thus can resolve all doubts. This assumption defines knowledge basically as so much fact-gathering and lacks any awareness whatsoever of the relational and contextual dimension of knowledge, and thus it is not surprising that the investigation of Lara's past yields only confusion or that the past dissolves into so much foreign gibberish to those who are trying to discover it. Words are pestilent—

they get in the way of every effort to know Lara's situation—because they develop out of actual social processes and then control what can be known about these processes. They are not equivalent with knowledge, but they are inextricably tied to ways of knowing; when thought becomes confused, so does language. The emphasis on words in the poem is a reflection of deep-seated contradictions at the center of Lara's world, contradictions that promote deceit and generate weakness at the deepest levels of culture, to the point finally of causing sweeping turmoil.[9]

The depiction of the past not only illustrates the absence of historical awareness in Lara's world. It also suggests the social impulse to escape present difficulties through an emotional investment in a far-removed, utopian sphere— the excitement over Lara's past takes society (at least imaginatively) away from the present. Not even Lara escapes this mindset, for he comes to believe under the pressure of the moment that his past, hidden from the world he despises, is preferable to the present. When he begins to understand the turmoil that characterizes feudal society at its most basic level, and when he realizes that he cannot easily lay this turmoil to rest, his response is identical to Conrad's, at least in spirit—he takes refuge in his thoughts of the past. As he lies dying, he and Kaled

> . . . spake of other scenes, but what—is known
> To Kaled, whom their meaning reach'd alone;
> And he replied, though faintly, to their sound,
> While gaz'd the rest in dumb amazement round.
> They seem'd even then—that twain—unto the last
> To half forget the present in the past;
> To share between themselves some separate fate,
> Whose darkness none beside should penetrate.
>
> (2. 446–53)

If, as Byron says in his advertisement to the poem, *Lara* can safely be regarded "as a sequel to *The Corsair*," then this view of the past becomes both interesting and problematic. Does Lara see in the past a world preferable to the world he presently inhabits? Does he wish to escape the world Conrad had longed to enter, to return to the world Conrad had longed to escape? Which past offers the possibility of true fulfillment, the one for which Lara longs or the one for which Conrad had longed? These questions are unanswerable because, in some respects, they are misdirected, formulated in the same uncritical terms that the narrative has established. The backward impulse evidenced by both Conrad and Lara is an escapist and utopian desire arising from the same source—the gross inadequacies of their respective situations. They do not look to the past because it holds out substantial hope for them, but because the present leaves them frustrated, isolated, and alienated. The past, as they dream of it, is an ideal, an imagined refuge from the present, and as such it both sustains them and controls them. For while it gives them a sense of purpose, a belief in something better than what present life offers, it also traps them into looking away from the social issues at hand for explanations—it substitutes nostalgia for analysis and action.

The attention given to these different, even contradictory, versions of the past offers a valuable insight into the larger context of ideas and beliefs that control the action of the story. That Lara's particular situation remains a mystery, despite the energetic public effort to uncover it, is merely symptomatic; it is only one manifestation of the pervasive inability of society, under the conditions presented in the poem, to know fully the character and content of social life. This negative portrayal of society, however, should not be viewed as simply another of Byron's many commentaries on human frailty and shortcoming. In fact, it does not reveal so much about absolute public ignorance as it does about the prevailing ideology that sets the limits of social life and thus determines what can and cannot be known. This ideology, the poem makes clear, is characterized mainly by abstract thinking, which obscures and distorts the substance of experience. While he never explains in detail the ideas governing Lara's world, Byron suggests repeatedly that their authority is linked directly to the traditions defining feudal society. The structures of authority located within these traditions are illustrated frequently, but perhaps are most apparent in the questions and speculations that Lara's persistent silence generates among the public:

> In him inexplicably mix'd appeared
> Much to be loved and hated, sought and feared.
> Opinion varying o'er his hidden lot,
> In praise or railing ne'er his name forgot;
> His silence formed a theme for others' prate—
> They guess'd—they gazed—they fain would know his fate.
> What had he been? what was he, thus unknown,
> Who walked their world, his lineage only known?
> A hater of his kind?
>
> (1. 289–97)

These questions point towards a distinction that is maintained through the entire narrative and that informs to a large extent the assumptions behind the narrative action—namely that between *tradition*, on one hand, with its abstract definitions of social life and, on the other, the actual *material conditions* that are hidden from view and out of which tradition develops. Throughout the story, position, name, law, custom, inheritance, lineage—in short, the ingredients that most explicitly identify feudal society are presented as commonplace, natural, insurmountable, and beyond dispute—Lara's lineage is known. These ingredients are made to represent the absolute context of social life in the poem; they are categories that appear to be constitutive of reality. But in fact they are abstractions, a reified version of actual social processes, and as abstractions they actively prevent characters from obtaining any real sense of the human conditions behind them, so that historical and social understanding is severely distorted.

That the abstract is made to represent the actual has powerful social implications, both as a means of social control and as a source of eventual social turmoil. The role of tradition, as it is presented in the poem, is to assure conformity of thought and belief, to shape society's perception both of the present and of the past, to give social order the appearance of universal purpose, coherence, and substance. This is accomplished, as the characterization of Lara attests, by obscuring the real relations, events, and struggles that form the actual base of society.

Writing in a different context, Raymond Williams focuses this social function of tradition: ". . . [T]radition is in practice the most evident expression of the dominant and hegemonic pressures and limits. . . . [I]ndeed it is the most powerful practical means of incorporation." It functions, among other means, by "discard[ing] whole areas of significance, or reinterpret[ing] or dilut[ing] them, or convert[ing] them into forms which support or at least do not contradict the really important elements of the current hegemony."[10] Or, as Williams has noted more recently: ". . . [T]radition . . . is self-evidently a process of deliberate continuity, yet any tradition can be shown, by analysis, to be a selection and reselection of those significant received and recovered elements of the past which represent not a necessary but a *desired* continuity."[11] In *Lara,* these ideas are everywhere apparent. The past cannot be known under the conditions prevailing in the narrative—it remains a mystery that cannot be deciphered—because the actual social and historical processes that would explain feudal life have been distorted or reinterpreted. Under feudalism social determinants are suppressed, consistently pushed out of the public mind, and replaced "by existing general social relations"[12] (for instance, lineage, inheritance, personal life) which then are passed off as the defining context of history. Thus it is that the public can know Lara's name and lineage and still know nothing.

The problem here is that there is a gross contradiction between the definition and the actual processes of history—human experience is not static, even if the definitions of it are. One obvious consequence of this prevailing system of thought, as evidenced by the extreme frustration of virtually every character, at every level of the social scale, is that in eliding the substance of the past it generates growing unrest, which eventually must press to the front of social life. The public attention given to Lara's situation, while illuminating the severe limitations of feudal culture, constitutes at the same time an impulse (however misdirected), even among the aristocracy, to overcome abstraction. It indicates the social need to understand the content rather than simply the form of human experience, and in this sense the mystery surrounding Lara corresponds to the actual human role in history. That the details of this role are hidden beneath an abstract rhetoric of tradition—and that existing conditions in fact depend upon ongoing ignorance—inevitably produces resistance and violence, as becomes explicit in the insurrection that erupts in the latter part of the story.

The extent to which such abstractions can control social life is suggested in the portrayal of the serfs. Burdened by a mystified past, the serfs are doomed to live in a mystified present, their contributions consistently minimized by a value system that celebrates only an aristocratic tradition. Even while they actively create the world portrayed in the narrative, even while their involvement in the various struggles and exchanges displays the actual substance of the social and historical processes, their presence never achieves significance beyond the most nebulous and personal considerations. Lara's "soul compassion knew" (2. 183) for them, but only as a ruler feels compassion for those over whom he exercises power. Kaled does not denigrate them, but neither can he "descend to them" (1. 573), presumably because he is fundamentally superior to them. They compose the armies fighting both for and against Lara; they compose the labor force which prepares the feast, serves at the carousals, and produces the physical necessities of life; they constitute the power of public order—they are the heart of social life, and yet the feudal priorities and values controlling their situation obscure their importance and even their presence.

The full significance of the confusion and misperceptions that surround social relations is suggested by the fact that in the tale everyone is implicated in the movements of society, drawn without exception into the struggles and controversy that arise through the course of the story. To return for a moment to the characterization of Lara, we may note that even in its compelling portrayal of the alienated Byronic hero, the narrative denies that individuals can in any substantive way achieve independence from social relations, insisting that private and social matters are in the final analysis the same. This point is graphically illustrated in the presentation of Lara's personal and public life, which he consistently fails to understand. When he returns to his homeland, he participates in the activities of his culture:

> Not unrejoiced to see him once again,
> Warm was his welcome to the haunts of men;
> Born of high lineage, link'd in high command,
> He mingled with the Magnates of his land;
> Join'd the carousals of the great and gay,
> And saw them smile or sigh their hours away.
>
> (1. 95–100)

Despite his sociable conduct, however, he does not perceive himself to be fully social, and in fact he reserves what be believes to be his true character to himself, understanding it in highly personal, even secretive terms. If he moves about in public, still he

> . . . did not share
> The common pleasure or the general care;
> He did not follow what they all pursued
> With hope still baffled, still to be renew'd;
> Nor shadowy honour, nor substantial gain,
> Nor beauty's preference, and the rival's pain:
> Around him some mysterious circle thrown
> Repell'd approach, and showed him still alone.

(1. 101–8)

It should be clear that this aloneness is not independence, even if Lara insists otherwise. It is, rather, a sign of his alienation, an indication of the extent to which his consciousness (like Manfred's after him) has become isolated. The narrative action elaborates fully the impossibility of Lara's escaping the demands that social life makes on all individuals, charting as it does a steady course whereby his assumptions of personal autonomy are carefully challenged and repeatedly undermined, until he is fully caught in a popular uprising. The only truly personal moment he experiences in the story is his death, and even this experience is in important ways mediated by the course of events which has produced it.

Read in this way, Lara's characterization indicates forcefully the unavoidable presence and power of social relations. In describing Lara, the narrative offers the clearest and most moving example of the Byronic hero, completely dislocated from the world, absorbed entirely by his own deep-seated confusions and sense of aloneness, and a "stranger" to everything around him (see especially 1. 313–60).[13] But, while all the ingredients of abstract characterization are carefully developed, at the same time the narrative makes Lara's personality directly dependent upon the explosive circumstances surrounding him. That neither Lara nor the other characters ever clearly perceives actions and systems of thought does not lessen the extent to which the many abstractions and portrayals of an ostensibly universal human condition arise from social relations. The swelling antagonism that finally erupts in the later sections of the narrative shows the insistent priority of the specific conditions of social life despite individual or even collective denials of them. Every description that contributes to the abstraction of Lara's character also exposes the material base upon which these abstractions rest.

Another way of understanding the powerful social network governing the narrative action is by considering the specific way Lara's position evolves through the poem. In an important respect Lara is very like Don Juan in that he never really initiates any action, but rather is acted upon or is drawn against his will into action by external pressures. He desires anonymity, peace, and privacy, a life apart from the community he inhabits; and he consciously separates himself from the mindset of status quo life. And yet he is consistently denied the comfort of his perceptions, and denied as well the attainment of his objectives. Not only is he the object of chatter by all classes of people, but he is also drawn into open conflict—Ezzelin makes a direct accusation, after which Otho challenges him to fight; and later Otho's army makes a direct attack on Lara. He is battered from every side by a world whose importance he denies and wishes to be rid of. The more obdurate he becomes—the more certain he is of his private character—the more viciously the world around him refuses him his independence. Despite his desire for peace, he can never escape or avoid the primary claim that his culture has on him, nor can he remain neutral in the face of events rumbling through society. He is forced to confront openly the situation that has alienated him.

The social implications of the contradictions evident in the characterization of Lara become most apparent in the insurrection. The scenes describing this episode illustrate powerfully that, when social attitudes become increasingly hardened and rigid rather than flexible, when the field of inquiry is narrowed rather than widened, the consequence inevitably will be destructive, both in personal and in social terms.

The social criticism implicit in the portrayal of this insurrection does not constitute a blanket condemnation of popular uprisings, but rather offers a judgment against the specific principles upon which the resistance of Lara and the serfs is grounded. The narrative states emphatically, for instance, that Lara's leadership is motivated by private rather than by political concerns, that it is an act of desperation rather than of liberation. Even when he releases his slaves from their "feudal fetters" (2. 216) his concern is not for their independence, which, indeed, he neither desires nor promotes. Alienated from his "rightful" class by Otho's fury, he turns to the people as a refuge from and as a defense against his enemy. He frees the serfs to obtain their loyalty and support in his personal quarrel with Otho:

> Cut off by some mysterious fate from those
> Whom birth and nature meant not for his foes,
> Had Lara from that night, to him accurst,
> Prepared to meet, but not alone, the worst.
> Some reason urged, whate'er it was, to shun
> Enquiry into deeds at distance done;
> By mingling with his own the cause of all,
> E'en if he fail'd, he still delay'd his fall.
> . . . .
> What cared he for the freedom of the crowd?
> He raised the humble but to bend the proud.
> (2. 234–41, 252–53)

As this selfish motive makes clear, he has not relinquished his aristocratic and feudal mindset, has not developed a substantive critique of the situation he faces, but rather has simply transferred his authority and sense of natural superiority to a separate sphere; in their view of power and of social life, Lara's attitudes are identical to Otho's and to those of other Byronic heroes. He is "inseparably bound" (2. 231) to the serfs for negative rather than for positive reasons, and thus his position is finally no different from, say, Selim's in *The Bride* or from Faliero's in *Marino Faliero*.[14]

The serfs, too, lack a political understanding of their situation. They are worn down by the tyranny exercised against them, increasingly resistant to the despots who have all but destroyed their hope, their integrity, and their possibility of community fulfillment. Their situation, they believe, demands substantive social change, and to this end "They waited but a leader" (2. 230), with Lara eventually stepping in to fill this important role. That they throw their support behind him suggests both their desperation and their insufficient grasp of events. They rally around Lara not so much because he abstains from tyranny, as because he has not been present to oppress them, and because during his short tenure as feudal chief he has displayed a "milder sway" (2. 172) than other lords. This is not to suggest that, left to himself, Lara in fact would be a tyrant of the same caliber as those who have generated popular discontent (though, to be sure, his selfishness in the insurrection might provide a good basis for such an argument), but simply that the serfs cannot know him, cannot know whether his objectives are to rectify serious social ills and to work for social amelioration or (as proves to be the case) to advance his own interests. In short, while the serfs are oppressed and desperately in need of social relief, they lack the political and class consciousness necessary to make their campaign successful. It is in the light of this ignorance that the cynicism surrounding this insurrectionary surge must be understood:

> That morning he [Lara] had freed the soil-bound slaves
> Who dig no land for tyrants but their graves!
> Such is their cry—some watchword for the fight
> Must vindicate the wrong, and warp the right:
> Religion—freedom—vengeance—what you will,—
> A word's enough to raise mankind to kill;
> Some factious phrase by cunning caught and spread
> That guilt may reign, and wolves and worms be fed!
>
>   (2. 218–25)

Viewed in this way, the insurrection, like the issues traced earlier in this chapter, is not a self-contained phenomenon but rather a part of the larger dialectic of social life. The important question surrounding the uprising is not whether Lara is malicious and manipulative, or whether the serfs, as members of the lower classes, are naturally ignorant, but rather what the conditions are within the narrative action that make this sort of fiasco possible, even unavoidable. The "political defeatism," of which Carl Lefevre speaks, certainly is one characteristic of Lara, and the result of Lara's position, as Lefevre rightly notes, is "utter oblivion."[15] But this need not be understood as a statement about the doomed human condition, or even, from a biographical perspective, about Byron's spiritual despair. The attitudes that are manifested in the insurrection are a *culmination,* a crystallization, of an array of issues and relations that infuse the narrative, and they cannot be reduced finally to purely psychological and personal concerns. The role of tradition, of language, of the past, of the physical structures underlying feudal society—these are the determinants that should be used to measure the final social chaos.

One point, mentioned above, bears stressing here and might help to clarify the full social dimension of the insurrection—namely, that the violence and chaos surrounding the uprising cannot be traced to a single source. The insurrection does not lend itself readily to straightforward causal analysis. To understand this we need only consider that Byron emphasizes equally the unrest at the top and at the bottom of the social scale. If the serfs have long experienced oppression, their situation alone is insufficient to stir military resistance. It takes Lara's quarrel with Ezzelin and Otho—an ostensibly personal disagreement between aristocrats—to bring unrest into public view. This emphasis does not deny the class dimension of the insurrection, but attempts to understand it in terms of the full range of conflicts encompassing the narrative action. The insurrection becomes inevitable because every facet of social life is inadequate; it cannot be explained simply as a conspiracy or as an isolated complaint, but must be seen as an eruption of all society into startling discord. This focus also helps to clarify the failure of the insurrection to change substantially feudal structures of authority, for it stresses that, while all of society is implicated in the action, social ignorance prevails. While class struggle stands at the center of social conflict, the narrative suggests that it cannot generate improved conditions in this instance because it is too narrowly perceived, never developing a broad and deep social awareness capable of penetrating the forces and relations that control social life. As the plight of both Lara and the serfs illustrates, the absence of social consciousness assures the failure of class resistance.

The steady deterioration of social conditions gradually affects every facet of human experience, including the religious. While in *Lara* Byron does not give religion as prominent a role as he had, say, in *The Giaour,* he nonetheless asserts its direct social relevance, indicating that the value and authority of religion depend heavily upon prevailing circumstances. Unlike in *The Giaour,* in which Byron had shown his hero retreating from society into a protective religious refuge, in *Lara* he has his hero flatly reject religion. This different handling does not so much indicate a radical shift of opinion about religion as suggest a shift of perspective and of narrative intention. *The Giaour* had focused on and elaborated the institutional role that religion can play, illustrating that the service provided by conventional religion does not always involve strictly spiritual considerations. In *Lara,* the brief picture of religion seems to be concerned

almost wholly with spiritual questions. The description of Lara's death emphasizes this point:

> Yet sense seem'd left, though better were its loss;
> For when one near display'd the absolving cross,
> And proffered to his touch the holy bead
> Of which his parting soul might own the need,
> He look'd upon it with an eye profane,
> And smiled—Heaven pardon! if 'twere with disdain;
> And Kaled, though he spoke not, nor withdrew
> From Lara's face his fix'd despairing view,
> With brow repulsive, and with gesture swift,
> Flung back the hand which held the sacred gift,
> As if such but disturbed the expiring man,
> Nor seem'd to know his life but *then* began,
> That life of Immortality, secure
> To none, save them whose faith in Christ is sure!
>
> (2. 476–89)

While Kaled rather than Lara emphatically and bitterly rejects the religious
offering, the passage makes clear Lara's absence of conviction as well. Their
positions reveal quite explicitly that, under the conditions that have come to
prevail, religion is emptied of whatever value it might otherwise have. In a
society where personal and public antagonisms tear at the very heart of life,
where ignorance breeds violence, where oppression and self-interest are primary
principles of life, spiritual comfort is impossible and spiritual truth is a sham. In
the face of the severe turmoil that has pervaded the story, Christianity becomes
just another institution, just another sign of what is wrong with feudal culture.
Although religion offers itself here as a pure, transcendent, and redemptive gift,
Lara's painful situation, surrounded by the awful events described in the story,
bitterly, viciously points up the ignorance that alone could see it in this light.
The oppressive reality that has become ever heavier through the narrative
refuses to exempt even religion from the network of social relations governing
Lara's world, compellingly illustrating its inability to stand outside the material
context of human experience.

Against the background of these large social issues, several plot-level episodes
which seem designed primarily to heighten the mystery and exotic tone of the
story take on an added significance and in fact become critical to a full
understanding of the power and complexity of the social relations being portrayed. Ezzelin's disappearance, for instance, makes explicit at the plot level what
virtually every other situation in the narrative suggests—namely, that the truth
of events is extremely elusive. While he drops several hints that the curious
night scene towards the conclusion of the story describes Ezzelin's murder, the

narrator carefully avoids direct statement, noting doubtfully of the object float-
ing in the stream that

> . . . the features of the dead,
> If dead it were, escaped the observer's dread;
> But if in sooth a star its bosom bore,
> Such is the badge that knighthood ever wore,
> And such 'tis known Sir Ezzelin had worn
> Upon the night that led to such a morn.
> If thus he perish'd, Heaven receive his soul!
>
> (2. 588–94)

The apparent murder that the narrator witnesses is described matter-of-factly
(see 2. 550–97), but the interpretation of it is speculative at best, a diffident,
poor attempt to construct a plausible explanation of a serious crime. That the
narrator fails to provide clear information in such a circumstance emphasizes
that even the most specific and isolated events are subject to ignorance and
mystification, capable of generating confusion rather than understanding.

Further, Ezzelin's disappearance reduces the credibility of purely individualist
perspectives on the narrative. The story had begun with an ordinary personal
disagreement between two aristocrats, which, we soon realize, is in fact symptomatic and illustrative of a much broader set of social questions. Through the
narrative, Byron steadily dismantles or surrounds with mystery the purely private
aspect of the action, giving ever-increasing attention to the conditions of social
life inscribed in the story. Ezzelin's disappearance, combined with Lara's death,
literally removes the individual issue that is ostensibly at the center of the
narrative, so that the discord pervading feudal culture stands more clearly in
view.

Perhaps the most important function, however, of the scene describing
Ezzelin's apparent murder is that it raises the gender issue again. In fact, this
scene marks an odd sort of reversal and elaboration of Leila's disappearance in
The Giaour. Just as Byron's first tale had presented the fisherman-narrator's
mysterious account of a body being tossed silently into the sea, this scene
presents a peasant's account of a body being dumped silently into a river. The
difference, however, is that in *The Giaour* the implication had been that Hassan
was disposing of a woman, while the implication here, according to most
readers,[16] is that a woman (Kaled) is disposing of a man. This radical difference
once more raises questions about the conventional assumptions governing the
personal and social roles of women, developing further an idea that had been
central in earlier tales.

The gender issue is given fullest expression in the scene near the end of the
story that addresses Kaled's identity directly. That her identity is of critical
significance in the narrative is evidenced by the fact that it is the only informa-

tion of substance that is ever revealed. While the earlier tales had offered conflicting views on the personal and public, the passive and active, roles of women and had tended to portray women in terms of various idealisms and hollow sentiments (recall, for instance, Leila, Zuleika, Medora, and Gulnare), *Lara* attempts to give a consistent and sympathetic portrayal of a nonidealized, active heroine. Until the final scenes, Byron portrays Kaled entirely in "masculine" terms, providing only hints of her true sex. One result of this characterization is to acknowledge a public identity for Kaled (albeit a subservient one). Her strangeness, it is assumed, is due to the fact that she is foreign rather than to the fact that she is a woman, so that she is able to enter public life in a way that the feminine characters in the other tales could not.

I am not suggesting that Byron at last had resolved the issue that had been central in all of the previous tales. In *The Siege of Corinth*, published after *Lara*, and in subsequent works as well, he returns to this matter, often with renewed confusion.[17] But *Lara* at least opens the field of inquiry by implying that masculine and feminine roles are not necessarily biologically determined in every case. Thus it is that, alienated from traditional assumptions and codes, Kaled is not bound to Lara simply by emotions, but by "heart and brain" (2. 537), and likewise that Lara displays a strong touch of so-called feminine emotionalism. Further, Kaled does not shy from physical violence or fear the burdens that belong apparently only to the masculine world (compare Medora or Zuleika on this point). In short, she and Lara represent a different kind of sexual relationship, founded on principles not sanctioned by the world in which they live. Her disguise emphasizes both her distance from accepted norms, and as well the particular qualities she has come to embrace. Again, the point here is not simply that women are really men, but rather that gender differences are often socially ascribed and defined, usually working to the detriment of women, as the earlier tales powerfully attest.

Every issue and idea in *Lara* is on some level socially engaged, illustrating McGann's assertion that the tale "makes the political dimension of the earlier poem [*The Corsair*] even more explicit" (*BCPW* 3:452). It is true, as I have stressed, that the tale gives us astonishingly little specific information. At the end of the story virtually the only detail we have learned is Kaled's identity. We do not know Lara's past, even though this seems to be the central focus of the story, nor do we know for sure what happens to Ezzelin, even though his disappearance sparks an insurrection. But this is precisely the poem's strength. By consistently withholding local details, the poem directs our attention steadily away from isolated or private matters to larger social concerns, projecting a dialectic of social life that subsumes all purely individual considerations. Thus, in the case of Lara, while we do not learn about his past, we do learn about the values, attitudes, and demands of the culture that assume the importance of his past; and in the case of Ezzelin, while we do not learn the details of his disappearance, we do learn about the cultural assumptions surrounding his disappearance. This larger social perspective helps to explain as well additional issues that otherwise seem unduly vague or piecemeal. The question of spiritual truth, as we have seen, is not as important in the tale as society's belief or disbelief in spiritual truth, nor is the natural role of women as important as what feudal culture believes their natural role to be. Understood in this way, even while the story lacks specific details, and even while it is governed very strongly by pessimism and gloom, in social and historical terms it is substantive, accurate, and even to some extent hopeful and liberating. Not only does the poem portray convincingly the complex dimensions and power of social relations, but, more importantly, in doing this it illustrates the severe limitations of purely individualist principles, thus allowing us to see the positive possibilities of a systematic social approach to the study of culture.

6

The Siege of Corinth

B YRON found *The Siege of Corinth* more difficult to write than any of his
previous four tales. Begun perhaps as early as 1812 (and perhaps even before
the composition of *The Giaour* [see *BLJ* 5:32]), *The Siege* was abandoned and
then resumed again in 1813, 1814, and early 1815, before being finally completed in October 1815.[1] This awkward compositional process, unusual for
Byron, drained him of any real interest in or regard for the poem, as is evidenced
by his scant attention to it in his letters and journals. As McGann notes, he
probably viewed it as "a patchwork" (*BCPW* 3:481) rather than as a consistent
and coherent narrative, and most subsequent critics have agreed that it is the
least successful of the Eastern Tales.[2]

While it is impossible to know with certainty why Byron found this particular
tale so difficult to write, even though in many respects it simply duplicates the
other, hastily written tales (in characterization, in style, in setting, and to some
degree in plot), it is likely that his compositional problems were conceptual and
intellectual in nature, arising from his attempt (never stated, but everywhere
implicit) to develop a poetic perspective grounded upon historical understanding. This is suggested not only by the fact that *The Siege* is the first of Byron's
narratives to situate its action within a specific historical context,[3] but also by
the fact that Byron started and abandoned other historical narratives during this
same period, for instance "Il Diavolo Inamorato" and "The Monk of Athos,"
both of which attempted to make use of the same general body of information
that finally contributed to *The Siege* and to *Parisina*. Moreover, during this period
he also began writing a version of *Werner*, a historical drama set during the
Thirty Years' War, and did not complete this work until 1822. Every attempt
during these years to combine history and poetry was extremely painful and,
more often than not, was unsuccessful as well.

The overwhelming difficulty Byron faced was not simply how to describe
historical events and episodes—he had done this successfully and with apparent
ease in *Childe Harold's Pilgrimage* 1–2—but rather how to *imagine* historical
processes at work, that is, how to treat systematically and fully the collective
pressures that constitute as well as shape both events and the individual experi-

ence of those events. Such a focus would relegate local details to secondary importance (and indeed in both *The Siege* and *Werner* Byron alters details occasionally) while stressing the priority of social structure. Further, it would make interpretation and conceptualization central to the poetic imagination, requiring that poetry be judgmental, analytical, and politically aware—a prospect that doubtless intimidated Byron at this point in his life, even while he was drawn to it.[4] *The Siege* clearly displays unease with such a poetic perspective; but, if the poem is not entirely successful as historical narrative—it is weakened by many of the same evasions that characterize the other tales—it nonetheless marks an important departure for Byron and indeed indicates the direction that most of his subsequent poetry would take.

In one respect, by establishing a specific historical groundwork for its narrative action, *The Siege* accomplishes what *The Giaour* had attempted but failed to do, and thus might be regarded as a semi-successful rewriting of the first tale along historical lines. When he published *The Giaour*, Byron appended a brief and self-conscious advertisement to the poem, noting the historical moment of the story, and this shows that he wanted to combine history and poetry. But, despite its compelling social dimension, the tale itself largely ignored historical specificity, proceeding almost randomly from one abstraction to another, suggesting Byron's inability or unwillingness to address historical issues head on. *The Siege* corrects this deficiency by placing its action fully within a discernible social situation that is kept consistently before the reader as the locus of action, so that each personality twist and each decision to act (or not to act) appears as an instance within a larger network of relations.

Byron's decision to write his first avowedly historical narrative about the 1715 siege of Corinth, despite the fact that he presumably knew relatively little about its historical background beyond what he had learned from conversations during his 1810 travels,[5] is significant for several reasons. On purely psychological grounds, it is possible that he settled on the siege because of its obscurity; because the episode was virtually unknown to the English reading public, there would be little chance of his being challenged by his critics on historical accuracy—an important consideration at a time when he was diffident and generally confused in the face of all political matters. Obscurity of subject matter also had the advantage of allowing him a flexibility that he would not have had with more widely treated subjects. In writing about the siege, his conceptual and interpretative interests were not at every turn put to the test of actual events, so that he retained a degree of the poetic autonomy he had found in the other highly exotic tales; the siege provided him with a historical perspective without insisting in every instance on the priority of specific, empirical evidence.

In intellectual terms, it is probable that Byron was drawn to the taking of Corinth because it represented a moment of severe social crisis and radical change. That he was fascinated by such historical moments on both grand and small scales is indicated not only in *Lara*, which depicts feudal society at a moment of extreme upheaval, but also in his later historical dramas, where the instant of social change becomes a consistent and paramount concern. The appeal of crisis periods may have been that they allowed him not only to intensify his poetic characters by delineating their strategies for dealing with inescapable and unusually critical situations, but also to suggest the larger and more encompassing pressures of collective human experience. That is, in narratives about historical or social crisis, as characters individually make their way as best they can against the obstacles before them, they lay bare not only the workings of their own psyches, but more importantly the dimensions and workings of their world. Under the fire of social upheaval, motivating assumptions and values stand exposed, and Byron increasingly found these to be compelling subject matter for his poetry.

Further, the siege would have been appealing for ideological reasons, for it allowed Byron to dramatize the claims and patterns of various systems of belief that would have been pitted against one another during this upheaval. The conflict he charts, after all, is not only between Turkish and Venetian armies, but also between cultures. The siege enabled him to handle this subject with greater precision than he had in his earlier tales, because it gave him a means of weighing conflicting moral and religious considerations against one another within an objectively measurable context. Even if the renegade Alp and the benign Francesca present their respective values abstractly, the historical framework insists upon the material bases and implications of their beliefs. By placing the narrative action within a real historical context, Byron provides a foil for abstract presuppositions and for overly sentimentalized versions of human value.

Finally, the siege was an excellent subject for historical narrative because it highlighted a common but often overlooked occurrence—namely, the way political struggle can destroy a historically unseen majority. The exchange between the Venetians and the Turks, it should be remembered, took place on foreign soil and involved masses of people who were innocent of the issues in contention. As George Finlay notes in his account of this conflict, the Venetian garrison at the time of the siege "was crowded with Greek families, who had retired with all their most valuable property within its walls. These non-combatants were all eager for a capitulation,"[6] which of course was never forthcoming. This detail reveals a terrifying fact—the siege had nothing to do with a struggle for liberty, with the defense of a people, or with any military cause that was even remotely justifiable. It involved only the blind struggle between enemy states for political domination, without regard for the expectations or rights of the actual citizens who lived in the disputed territory. While Byron does not focus directly on the literal sacrifice of these innocent citizens, he makes it central by implication. By focusing on the stubborn and violent standoff between states, he throws into relief the absurdity and full-scale destruction that actually define the situation—as he cynically tells the story, political struggle arising solely from a desire for power or from purely private motives, rather than from social need, destroys *everything*, irrespective of class, belief, or heritage.

That Byron was not entirely up to the challenge that his subject posed (see, for instance, the many complaints by Murray and Gifford about his stylistic shortcomings, or note the charges leveled by contemporary reviewers of the poem)[7] does not lessen the importance nor even indeed the power of the poem. Although his execution is often technically sloppy, too mechanical, and overly systematic, he nevertheless introduces and defines in surprisingly clear fashion categories of thought that had been inadequately conceived in his previous tales. He does not avoid the abstractions and sentiments of the earlier tales, but casts them more clearly within a framework that can explain them. In *The Siege* he displays unprecedented control of his conceptual materials, carefully establishing and ordering a finite set of issues and then attempting to present them as historically valid by having them embody and reflect the central conflict in the narrative between the Turks and the Venetians.

Byron's treatment of relations and ideas within society is here in many respects similar to his presentation in the earlier tales.[8] For instance, he begins by consciously omitting pieces of the social puzzle, the effect of which is to surround the narrative with mystery and, more importantly, to suggest the complexity of social analysis. Here, as previously, he denies our ability to know every detail of the past, not to suggest that history is unknowable, but to establish a particular kind of perspective, one which places priority on the historical moment and on its absorbing, untranscendable structures. We know of Alp's lineage, of his dissatisfaction with his country, and even of his "memory of a thousand wrongs" (83), but still, because these are abstractions rather than specifics, we cannot construct a mechanical set of causes and effects to explain his exile. To understand the situation at hand we are forced to examine the processes of social life that surround him and to conceptualize the relations that bind him. This method of presentation not only emphasizes "the present as history,"[9] but also decenters the narrative, denying the priority of a linear explanation of events and of individualist perspectives on events without denying the priority of historical context, and it throws into relief the components of the prevailing system.

Within this narrative framework of structural rather than causal analysis, the most consistently handled and far-reaching assumption is that social life becomes dangerous when its ruling ideas become abstracted from actual political and historical imperatives and from fundamental human needs. Byron approaches this matter from various perspectives, sometimes illustrating the pervasiveness of simple-minded abstract thought in the world of the poem, sometimes showing how it obscures social awareness and threatens social stability, but always insisting upon its connection in the last instance to material conditions. He measures the ideas that govern social life against carefully delineated (if occasionally overstated) material circumstances in a way that not only elaborates the frequent contradictions between value systems and social relations, but also shows how controlling ideas can be used to perpetuate social tyranny and oppression, even to the extent of jeopardizing social life itself.[10]

Two issues which are central in the earlier tales as separate concerns are united here to illustrate more forcefully than before the nature and volatile, destructive potential of sheer abstraction—namely, the place of women and of religion in society. As a transcendent being, Francesca surpasses earlier heroines (Leila, Zuleika, and Medora) in that she is presented literally as a disembodied spirit (see 478–500), the representation of all that is noble and good—she takes on an unmistakably allegorical significance. (And in typical Byronic fashion, Alp is presented as the time-bound mortal—"coop'd in clay"[11]—who projects onto her all of his highest spiritual yearnings and moral sense, seeing her as the one justification for living.) Setting aside for a moment feminist considerations of this situation, we can note that her ethereal presence—unlike that of her predecessors—is directly linked to Christianity; she is not only its spokesperson, but also a model of the hope and transhistorical purity that (the poem suggests) Christianity claims for itself. When she encounters Alp outside the Venetian garrison she speaks emphatically from religious conviction, admonishing him from the very start for having fallen "away from thy father's creed," and asking him to "sign / The sign of the cross" (531–33).

What goes unstated here is that her beauty and her religiosity, however innocent and abstract they appear, are in fact time-bound and committed (intentionally or not) to specific political positions. The creed to which she subscribes is explicitly a creed of national bounds—it does not admit the spiritual or moral integrity of Moslems, for instance—and it clearly supports pursuits of territorial acquisition (in this instance, the occupation of the Morea). Further, as the daughter of Minotti, governor of Corinth, she is directly tied to the Venetian instruments of rule and is as much a spokesperson for it as for Christianity. In fact, her politics, her religion, and even her sense of personal identity are finally indistinguishable, equal components in a single system of cultural power—her religion is orthodox; her patriotism is unquestioning; her commitment to her father is unbounded; and her belief that resistance to any of these is heresy of the first order is unshakable. Her position, at every turn, is charged with social significance, making absolute claims not only about spiritual but also about worldly matters highly suspect. As she commands Alp:

> . . . that turban tear
> From off thy faithless brow, and swear
> Thine injured country's sons to spare,
> Or thou art lost; and never shalt see
> Not earth—that's past—but heaven or me.
>
> (585–89)

This makes explicit what had been presented obliquely in *The Bride*, namely that love—however transcendent, noble, and even spiritual it appears—is never contextless, but is caught within particular and knowable constraints, and committed to specific political interests.

That Alp fails to see or to understand Francesca's unyielding social commitments, and the connections between these and her religious beliefs, does not establish Francesca's innocence of social reality; it demonstrates Alp's entrapment in the web of abstractions spun by the culture that he seeks to escape. To illustrate the degree of his misapprehension of circumstance we might consider his specific objectives with respect to Francesca. His sense of his situation is very similar to the lovesick shepherd's in pastoral literature. He believes that through sheer individual will he can reject all social contingencies that are not to his liking, while preserving and making a commitment to certain of society's objects (i.e., Francesca). As he tells Francesca's spirit, in language reminiscent of Marlowe:

> But thee will I bear to a lovely spot,
> Where our hands shall be joined, and our sorrow forgot.
> There thou yet shalt be my bride,
> When once again I've quelled the pride
> Of Venice.
>
>   (542–46)

This pastoral ideal (a good example of what William Empson calls the Romantic "cult of independence")[12] is undermined not so much by the "time" and fading flowers with which Raleigh counters Marlowe as by historical and political reality. Under the pressure of the actual situation at hand, Alp's speech is little more than self-aggrandizing wish-fulfillment, because the social struggle for power (despite Alp's denial of its priority or even existence) neither excepts nor excuses anything, not even love, a fact that Alp, to his own peril, never understands.

Before exploring further the broader social implications of the values associated with Francesca, I wish here to consider very briefly the poem's depiction of her as Alp's love interest and as an embodiment of a specific religious attitude. In one clear respect, her characterization is damnable ("what one would expect from a male author"), for she is presented as at once the kind of woman that every man dreams of (as an *object* of devotion), and as a representative of orthodox political and religious values; neither role says much in favor of the independence, integrity, and fundamentally human dimension of women. From a historical perspective, however, her characterization is precise and sympathetically drawn, showing her to be as much a victim of social contradiction and abstraction as Alp—a fact that Byron reveals without resorting to sentimental descriptions and assertions. Even while her characterization *expresses* social assumptions about women—that they are on one hand transcendentally pure and on the other the very voice of authority and oppression—at the same time it *reveals* the social tyranny over women by underscoring the values of a comprehensive and essentially patriarchal network of social relations. That Francesca mouths these values, that she cannot extricate herself from her circumstances or see the determinations and implications of her own beliefs, is not so much a sign of natural feminine weakness (she understands as much—or as little—as Alp, her male counterpart) as it is a sign of the power of ideology— her situation is not transparent, but mediated by circumstance; her roles are not self-chosen, but socially determined. For this reason, her fate (like Alp's) is directly bound to the fate of her culture, and her unenviable position (or, more generally, the position of women) cannot be changed until social conditions change. From this perspective, she is not simply an instance of the one-dimensional woman that men insist on seeing; she is a specific, human instance of how social oppression works, an example of how one person lives out the values and assumptions of her culture.

That the religious values presented initially in terms of Francesca's demeanor and beliefs are not finally a matter of simple personal conviction is evidenced in the descriptions of the world surrounding her, in which religion is portrayed as an active and central controlling force within society. If in The Giaour religion is described as a more or less passive institution that neatly absorbs the contradictions and pressures of everyday experience by focusing on an overriding and undefiled spiritual power, in The Siege it is presented as a multidimensional institution and ideology that contributes directly to the workings of political life, not only mirroring society's noblest principles (embodied in Francesca) but also betraying the actual practices that often stand behind those principles. The narrative events that illustrate this aspect of religion do not look back to earlier tales but forward to The Deformed Transformed, in which Byron sets the climactic and most violent military encounter within the walls of a church, brilliantly illustrating the horror that religious power can generate. In The Siege, the depiction of Christianity proceeds steadily from the idealized and noble presence of Francesca, to her call to religious authority, and finally to the interior of the church, where the final battle is fought. The presentation of war inside the church is in itself striking, but in Byron's hands it is also blackly ironic, savagely exploding conventional notions of religious innocence. The effect of the scene is not simply to show that religion, contrary to what people think, is actually bad for society; more to the point, it details the social interestedness of religion and the kind of life that religious values can support.

The narrative action challenges in several ways the absolute authority associated with Christianity. First, by idealizing Francesca, by presenting Alp as a self-described renegade, and by depicting the Turks as the invaders of a Christian stronghold, it concedes fully the ostensible moral superiority of the Christians in the story. Having described the external trappings of the situation, however, it proceeds to suggest the incongruities and contradictions boiling beneath. For one thing, as the history of the situation makes clear, this was a struggle for domination rather than for religious freedom; religion is simply one of the ideological weapons that the Venetians used in their struggles against the Turks.

Further, even while the Turks are the aggressors in this particular scene, within the larger historical context they are no different from the Venetians; both are ravaging a countryside that does not belong to them. In such a situation, Christian values are deeply and inescapably embroiled in political warfare, as responsible for, and as willing to shed, blood as the most hostile of enemies. This is powerfully illustrated in the description of Minotti inside the church:

> Darkly, sternly, and all alone,
> Minotti stood o'er the altar stone.
> Madonna's face upon him shone,
> Painted in heavenly hues above,
> With eyes of light and looks of love;
> And placed upon that holy shrine
> To fix our thoughts on things divine,
> When pictured there, we kneeling see
> Her, and the boy-God on her knee,
> Smiling sweetly on each prayer
> To heaven, as if to waft it there,
> Still she smiled; even now she smiles,
> Though slaughter streams along her aisles:
> Minotti lifted his aged eye,
> And made the sign of a cross with a sigh,
> Then seized a torch which blazed thereby;
> And still he stood, while, with steel and flame,
> Inward and onward the Mussulman came.
>
> (902–19)

In addition to the glaring contradiction here between the Madonna's unflinching beatific smile and the sweeping gore that this smile is cast upon, we learn a few lines later that the Venetian artillery had been stored all along beneath the church, in its burial vaults: "Here, throughout the siege, had been / The Christians' chiefest magazine" (936–37). There is of course a sledgehammer irony working here, with the venerable church resting comfortably upon weapons meant for human destruction; but there is also a symbolic (though admittedly not very sophisticated) handling of Christian values in all this. The power at the core of Christian virtue is finally a physical, even military power; though deeply submerged and hidden beneath the eternal smile of the Madonna, and out of view of the disembodied spirituality of Francesca, sheer physical strength is finally the security of a professedly passive religion. In this savage scene of slaughter we are made aware that Christianity and physical violence are, and always have been, so intricately tied as to be inseparable. Looking beyond its own self-representations to the history of this Christian stronghold, we learn that its

> . . . vaults beneath the mosaic stone
> Contained the dead of ages gone;
> Their names were on the graven floor,
> But now illegible with gore;
> The carved crests, and curious hues
> The varied marble's veins diffuse,
> Were smeared, and slippery—stained, and strown
> With broken swords and helms o'er thrown.
> There were dead above, and the dead below.
>
> (920–28)

Such descriptions as these, again, do not reflect the insincerity of, say, Francesca, or of any other individual Christian in the story; rather, they focus the much larger social and historical dimension of Christianity, suggesting that whatever any given individual accepts to be true in spiritual matters, and whatever the self-representation of a religious position may be, spirituality itself is always socially mediated, bound specifically to the larger interests and objectives of culture.

If Christianity never escapes the physical struggles of human experience and in fact often participates in some of the more violent episodes of history, this is because it has much more than spiritual truth at stake—it also has claims on much of earth's material wealth. The Venetian interest in the Morea was not simply altruistic, motivated by a missionary zeal to save a people from the hands of infidels. To judge from Byron's description of the church within the Venetian garrison, much could be gained from religious commitment; describing the Turk's invasion of the church, he notes:

> . . . from each other's rude hands wrest
> The silver vessels saints had blessed.
> To the high altar on they go;
> Oh, but it made a glorious show!
> On its table still behold
> The cup of consecrated gold;
> Massy and deep, a glittering prize,
> Brightly it sparkles to plunderers' eyes:
> . . . .
> And round the sacred table glow
> Twelve lofty lamps, in splendid row,
> From the purest metal cast;
> A spoil—the richest, and the last.
>
> (949–56, 962–65)

In such a setting as this, it becomes obvious that spiritual truth is not the only sacred concern of the Christians; gold plays its part as well. Just as a history of violence stands behind the Christian position (symbolized most clearly by

Christ's blood, "Which his worshippers drank," 959), material acquisition en-
cases it.

The effect of this portrayal of religion is not simply to demonstrate Christian
hypocrisy (though it does this) but more importantly to dramatize the material
history and context of all belief. The Moslems come off no worse than the
Christians (but no better, either). The error of Christianity as Byron presents it
is not that it believes in something, but that its belief system elides much of
human experience and that this suppressed experience refuses to lie still. To
separate truth and morality from human practice is not to assign them to a noble
sphere, though this is what the Venetian Christians would claim and (if Francesca is representative) believe, but rather to mystify the particular interests
exercised by the institutional representatives of truth and morality. When Alp is
held morally blameworthy because he has abandoned his homeland, or when the
Turks are held morally blameworthy because their system of belief and conduct is
predicated upon non-Christian principles, the issue in question is not finally
eternal or transcendental truth, but specific, even national claims about power—
who controls what, and by what authority do they control it? While Byron's
treatment of religion is not as clearly thought out as it is in his later works (for
instance, as in *The Deformed Transformed* and in *Werner*), it indicates his
understanding of the way religion serves the needs and objectives of specific
social interests.

The portrayal of religion provides a necessary basis for examining other issues
in the story, because it establishes the framework of thought that governs social
life. By playing Christianity against itself rather than, say, only against Moslem
belief, Byron focuses the *internal* character of social (and even individual) unrest
and alienation; that is, the real enemy of social stability is shown to be not some
hostile outside force, but rather the constituent elements of society itself,
specifically the relations between ideas and actualities. The implication of this
social perspective for other aspects of the world being portrayed is evidenced
readily in the discussions of history that are scattered through the narrative.
Faced with the prospect of violence, Alp, the night before his planned invasion
of Corinth, wanders from his camp into the serene night air and contemplates
the differences between past times and his own day. The most striking fact about
his reveries is not so much that he views the present as degraded beside the
glories of the past, but that his view of the past is fundamentally contradictory.
For instance, as would be expected, his first thoughts of the past are unreflec-
tingly idealistic, given to unreserved acknowledgment of the glories that no
longer are possible. The heroes of the past

> . . . fell devoted, but undying;
> The very gale their names seemed sighing:
> The waters murmured of their name;
> The woods were peopled with their fame;

> The silent pillar, lone and grey,
> Claimed kindred with their sacred clay;
> Their spirits wrapp'd the dusky mountain,
> Their memory sparkled o'er the fountain;
> The meanest rill, the mightiest river
> Rolled mingling with their fame for ever.
>
> (361–70)

That this view of history must suppress actual circumstances gradually becomes apparent as Alp wanders through the gore and blood of the day's battle. Such ugly sights as those before him raise the possibility that the past was not all glorious and make him understand that in fact it was probably subject to the same horrors as those dogging the present. As he plods through violent surroundings over corpses in a setting of almost surrealistic horror, the past comes to be drawn in very different terms:

> There is a temple in ruin stands,
> Fashioned by long forgotten hands;
> Two or three columns, and many a stone,
> Marble and granite, with grass o'ergrown!
> Out upon Time! it will leave no more
> Of the things to come than the things before!
> Out upon Time! who for ever will leave
> But enough of the past for the future to grieve
> O'er that which hath been, and o'er that which must be:
> What we have seen, our sons shall see;
> Remnants of things that have passed away,
> Fragments of stone, reared by creatures of clay.
>
> (450–61)

These lines concede the real horrors and insurmountable obstacles that always have plagued human experience, and they attempt to describe what all of human history must hold for man—defeat and despair. This assessment, however, is finally as simplistic as the previous glorification of the past, offering nothing more than a contradiction of blind idealization. Seeing the past as absolutely ruinous, after all, is no more specific or accurate than seeing it as absolutely noble; both positions fail to accommodate particular turns and twists of historical development.

As the events of the narrative show, neither of these perspectives tells us very much about the actual structures or meanings of history. But they tell us a great deal about the limitations of thought in a completely privatized world and, specifically, about Alp's staggering confusion in the face of an alienating network of relations (the description of Alp's response to these contradictory readings of history is telling: "He sate him down at a pillar's base, / And passed his hand athwart his face," 462–63). The problem of the past is identical to the problem of Christianity; it arises from the quantification, externalization, and abstraction of human experience, from a fact/value dichotomy that fails to see that every personal assessment of events involves a public value system, that even the most private perspectives have both social origin and social consequence.

This adds significantly to the earlier tales, which had blandly praised the past and condemned the present (see, for instance, the opening lines of *The Giaour*). While *The Siege* begins with this idea, it immediately undermines it by recasting the issue in terms of a particular set of values incapable of judging the past because it fails to grasp its own historical dimension. This handling historicizes the issue itself by focusing not on what the past actually means but rather on how versions of the past are created by the present and on the interests that the past is made to serve. This approach focuses more sharply the narrative's interest in the structure of social life with which the characters are forced to contend.

The problem of history—of its meaning, scope, and demands—is directly connected to the problem of external nature, which is likewise perceived abstractly and shown to be subject to the same contradictory interpretations. When Alp wanders alone outside his camp the night before the siege, he is struck by the profound beauty and uplifting presence of his physical surroundings. In a moment of Wordsworthian inspiration which anticipates the attitudes of Cain, a later Byronic renegade, Byron describes his hero's setting:

> . . . on the brow
> Of Delphi's hill, unshaken snow,
> High and eternal, such as shone
> Through thousand summers brightly gone,
> Along gulf, the mount, the clime;
> It will not melt, like man, to time.
> Tyrant and slave are swept away,
> Less formed to wear before the ray;
> But that white veil, the lightest, frailest,
> Which on the mighty mount thou hailest,
> While tower and tree are torn and rent,
> Shines o'er its craggy battlement.
>
> (319–30)

Nature, like spiritual truth, like Francesca's purity, or like past glories, is described as an external constant, as a mythic structure that is always superior to the toils of daily human life. And, as in Shelley's "Mont Blanc," although its power, overarching beauty, and unlimited freedom occasionally can be glimpsed, they are finally impenetrable, forever eluding humanity.

This view of nature, like the description of the past, collapses almost as soon as it is presented, undergoing a virtual transmogrification as the "tideless sea, / Which changeless rolls eternally" (381–82) gives way to a scene of utter horror that is not attributable to man alone. The carnage surrounding Alp is the result of human violence against humanity, to be sure, but the disturbing fact about the scene is that this carnage is ravenously set upon by nature itself:

> . . . he [Alp] saw the lean dogs beneath the wall
> Hold o'er the dead their carnival,
> Gorging and growling o'er carcass and limb;
> They were too busy to bark at him!
> From a Tartar's skull they had stripp'd the flesh
> As ye peel the fig when its fruit is fresh;
> And their white tusks crunch'd o'er the whiter skull,
> As it slipped through their jaws, when their edge grew dull,
> As they lazily mumbled the bones of the dead,
> When they scarce could rise from the spot where they fed;
>
> . . . .
> The scalps were in the wild dog's maw,
> The hair was tangled round his jaw.
> But close by the shore, on the edge of the gulf,
> There sat a vulture flapping a wolf
> Who had stolen from the hills, but kept away,
> Scared by the dogs, from the human prey.
>
> (409–18, 426–31)

While these descriptions are savage to the point of revulsion, they should not be dismissed as simply an instance of Byron's penchant for melodrama,[13] because they serve as a powerful antidote to naive celebrations of beatific nature.[14] But, again, the effect is not to suggest that the view of nature as red in tooth and claw is absolutely right, while the Wordsworthian picture of nature (at least as Byron understood it) is absolutely wrong. Rather, as with the treatment of history, it is to place Alp within a framework of thought that perceives only the contradictory possibilities within phenomena, and to emphasize that he has no satisfactory means of solving them.

In each of the four categories I have discussed—women, religion, history, nature—internal contradictions are of paramount importance and are presented with ever-increasing intensity as the tale proceeds. And in every case these contradictions provide a commentary on social life. While in one respect it is probably true to say that *The Siege* here demonstrates an extreme relativism by showing that any personal or social attitude is subject to contradiction and that therefore no perspective, ultimately, is tenable (a position that would be in keeping with Byron's general political confusion at this time), this does not seem to me to account sufficiently for what is happening in the tale. As I have tried to illustrate, the contradictions that appear throughout do not describe the essence of social reality, but rather offer a compelling commentary on a specific network of relations and ideas and a description of their far-reaching social implications;

the contradictions are a reflection of social processes rather than an abstract statement about them; they are a symptom of a problem rather than the problem itself. And, because in each instance they are socially determined (as is shown by the workings of the power relations governing the world of the poem), they also actively shape society, even while they reflect it. The conflict between the Venetians and the Turks is in many ways simply a literal display of these contradictions in action, a plot-level dramatization of the deeply imbedded ideological struggles that contribute significantly to the fate of an entire culture.

Having established Byron's narrative method and the tale's social perspective, it is possible to speak with some authority about Alp, in some respects the most Byronic (that is, the most abstractly drawn) of Byron's heroes. He is a powerful model of the Byronic renegade—he defies his homeland, his religion, and all authority; further, his past is mysterious and his superiority to his fellow man is obvious and unquestioned.[15] These characteristics are, I believe, directly related to the kind of world he lives in and in fact embody the same kinds of conflict and contradiction that are shown between Venice and Turkey at the political level.

One of the most striking features about Alp—and about all of the Byronic heroes—is that, despite his defiance, his distance from received social standards, or even his mysterious and brooding personality, he displays an ongoing connection to orthodox values, even at the moment he loudly rejects them. This idea connects directly to everything suggested previously. From the beginning of the story, we are told that Alp has not only exiled himself from his country, but even has borne arms against it, self-consciously adopting the objectives, the dress, and even the religious posture of the Turks; the emphasis is on the injustices he has suffered at the hands of his native culture and on his total rejection of the sources of these injustices. Through the course of the narrative, however, it becomes obvious that his rejection is not as absolute as it might at first appear; his attachment to Francesca is not, after all, a simple love interest, but indeed an attachment to a set of ideals and principles that Francesca represents for him. That is, he would reject the outward form of his highest beliefs (institutional religion, political commitment, nationality) while at the same time retaining their core assumptions and essential values as these are manifested in Francesca. He does not want to be a Moslem rather than a Christian, or a Turk rather than a Venetian; he wants to exercise Christian and Venetian values without the bother and the insults that come with their practical, institutional existence. It is this confusion—rather than his superiority—that gives his character its peculiar distance and allure, for it suggests at once the power of ideology over him (he embraces a given set of values at the deepest level even while he self-consciously rejects it)[16] and at the same time the blatant inadequacy of the values at the center of that ideology.

From this perspective, Alp's powerful and egotistical rejection of a world that has wronged him is a sign of isolation and alienation, not of strength. The contradictions pervading his world are not self-constituting realities that validate his discontent—the issue here is not simply that the world is a sham—but rather the conditions of social life that he must face; they provide the ideological and material framework for the historical moment in which he lives. The contradictions in his character are the contradictions of his world, and his increasing frustration and desperation are a sign that his world provides ever fewer avenues for human expression. His response to his situation might be described as an instance of "the disinheritance of consciousness,"[17] that is, as evidence of the diminishing space for the pursuit of human fulfillment in a world that has become fundamentally hostile. His struggles, like Manfred's after him, are the actions of a highly conscious and independent thinking individual seeking to find a domain that allows human integrity and freedom. What he faces without interruption is a world divided down the middle, compartmentalized, completely privatized. History is glorious, or else it is the record of decay; nature is beautiful, or else it is a field for open slaughter; love is pure and spiritual, or else it is committed wholeheartedly to state and political authority. The "freedom" of individuals in a world so constituted is to choose between these grating oppositions—one can be an idealist or a realist, an adherent of spiritual truth or a worldly-wise cynic.

The problem with a world divided along such rigid lines is of course that the choices make one either a complete conformist or a complete alien; neither position offers the possibility of real and productive social participation capable of generating human betterment. Further, it locates the complex issue of choice within a wholly private and individual context, which can in no way affect the social dimension of power relations. That is, it does not matter in such a world what Alp chooses, because the political, religious, emotional, and intellectual categories remain unchanged and even unchallenged. This is freedom without power. It is this mechanical world with its static and smothering structures that drives Alp to violent reaction; a world that allows no positive contribution, positive resistance, or participation in the social exercise of power assures violence as an expression of individual discontent.

At every turn the story is characterized by conflict and struggle; from the most private to the most obviously political levels (exemplified respectively by Alp and by the war between the Venetians and the Turks) the world being dramatized is rocked by internal division. Values are assumed to be independent of experience; individuals are assumed to be distinct from culture; culture itself is assumed to be distinct from nature. The inevitable conclusion towards which such a world must move is full-scale chaos, and this is precisely what the narrative describes. The story is not finally just about individual alienation, or even about social injustice, at least in the conventional sense of calculated oppression of individuals. It is about a culture at the moment of self-destruction and about the sources of that self-destruction.

In the tale's final, gruesome scene, in which the entire Venetian garrison is exploded, all of the images and interests of the earlier sections in the story are collected and subjected to inescapable violence.[18] The one act of unity in the story is a unity of death and destruction. When the garrison explodes, all differences which before had been cause for disturbance are annihilated: Turks and Venetians, Christians and Moslems, individuals and society, leaders and followers. Further, the human disaster echoes through the natural landscape, making a direct and powerful impact on it—the chaos of social life is reflected in the chaos of nature. Finally and ironically, this pervasive chaos leaves no basis for judging events, for measuring the worth of human situations: "Thus was Corinth lost and won" (1034). The pressures which once had weighed so heavily on Alp and on his world at last are removed, and yet there is no individual or social relief.

The Siege is perhaps more pessimistic than the earlier tales in that it depicts the collapse of an entire culture, but it is at the same time intellectually (if not technically) superior to them, because it refuses to linger over the possibility of an ideal sphere that might rescue one from the acknowledged divisions and horrors of experience. In each of the preceding tales, the idealisms that were being criticized were at the same time nostalgically admired, but here they are categorically condemned, shown to be ultimately as deadly as any enemy of humanity can be. Further, the individualist nature of these ideals is subordinated to a more direct and convincing social interest at the plot level. Alp is similar to Selim in that he dies at the moment he stops to consider the fate of Francesca, but, unlike in the earlier tale, this action occurs prior to the climactic scene. After the death of Alp, the tale moves fully into a dramatization of the social dimension of the action. The issues, which before had been described almost entirely in terms of Alp, are now presented in terms of the larger struggles, so that the destruction of society cannot be attributed to him alone. The violence and defeat that we witness in the final episodes result from a social structure grounded upon contradictory principles, that is, upon principles that do not meet the fundamental material, emotional, spiritual, and intellectual needs of its people.

7

Parisina

L IKE *The Siege of Corinth, Parisina* was written over an extended period (probably from 1812 to 1815) and was another product of Byron's frustrated efforts to write narrative poetry about a real historical event. Drawn from the same general body of historical material as *The Siege,* the poem is a sign both of Byron's determination to continue the project he had begun with the earlier narrative and of the importance that he attached to historical poetry (despite his many disclaimers about the value of *any* poetry).[1] That the difficulties of composition were at least as great as before, if not greater, is suggested by the fact that Byron twice lifted lines from his as yet incomplete manuscript and sent them to Isaac Nathan to be published with *A Selection of Hebrew Melodies,* a sure indication that he believed the historical material which had occupied him for more than three years would never be shaped into a complete and coherent narrative.[2] When he did at last finish the poem in late 1815, shortly after completing *The Siege,* he looked upon it with the same indifference that had accompanied completion of the previous poem, displaying very little emotion towards it, except in his insistence that it not be given separate publication (see, for instance, *BLJ* 5:13, or *BCPW* 3:489).

Despite the circumstances surrounding its composition, *Parisina* is, like *The Siege,* better than Byron admitted, and in fact it is perhaps the most successful of the Eastern Tales.[3] Certainly it is the most sophisticated in terms of historical perspective. Here, as before, Byron's emphasis is not so much on empirical data as on the ideas, assumptions, and values surrounding a particular historical situation. And, again, he demonstrates his willingness to subordinate or even to alter slightly particular details to emphasize these larger, superstructural concerns. While he announces in the Advertisement that Gibbon's *Miscellaneous Works* is the source of information for the narrative, in fact he simply uses Gibbon (as McGann puts it) "as the basis for a free poetic adaption of the actual events" (*BCPW* 3:490); the actual historical situation provides an objective context for his own idiosyncratic investigations into society.[4]

Byron doubtless was attracted to Gibbon's story initially for psychological reasons (i.e., because of his fascination with incest), and certainly the poem has a deeply personal tone which gives it an intensity unmatched by the earlier narratives.[5] But in his handling of this subject, he makes the poem more than a dramatization of a psychological obsession, though this is an undeniably powerful interest. The incest theme is important not only because it creates overwhelming and debilitating personal confusion, but also because it calls social power and values visibly into play. That is, it is not incest, but the ruling voices (physical and ideological) to which incest is made to answer that stand at the center of the narrative. Indeed, the intense psychological issues in the narrative take on their particular meanings because of (rather than in spite of) the political and social context in which they appear. In short, incest is not a constitutive concern, but rather is merely symptomatic of more far-reaching and deeply embedded social issues.

The social world described here looks very much like the worlds of the other tales, first because Byron uses the same tactic of dramatizing a moment of severe crisis in an attempt to lay bare the multiple personal and public forces at work in society. (In this case, as he notes in the Advertisement, he presents the relatively obscure "domestic tragedy" involving the family of the Marquis of Este in the early fifteenth century.) Further, he emphasizes the same general institutions, values, and problems that had dominated previous tales: religion, the state, political hierarchy, physical violence, crime, and so on. The image patterns used to set the tone of the poem are also standard. In the beginning, nature is described (though more briefly than before) as an ideal beauty that overarches the transience and turmoil of everyday life, only to be redefined later on in violent, alienating terms (compare, for instance, 1–14 to 93–99). Love, too, is understood at once as a transhistorical constant (as in the Hugo-Parisina relationship) and as a source of tragedy and despair (as in the Azo-Parisina relationship), evoking directly the conflict that had been central in *The Siege*, and, to a lesser extent, in *The Bride*. Finally, Byron again creates a hero whose total devotion to a woman places him at odds with society and who dies unrepentant in his love for this woman. While the presentation is visibly sharper and more carefully developed than before, the strategy seems unchanged—the poem comes across as a statement on the rigid and permanent oppositions that plague human experience.

In fact, however, there are important and very subtle changes that make this a radically different kind of poem. For one thing, Byron extends the social interest in the tale by giving serious attention to family life, a subject completely omitted in all of the previous tales, except *The Bride* and *Lara*, in which it is drawn but sketchily. The subject matter of course makes this focus inevitable, but Byron's handling of it is significant for the poem's social interest in at least two ways. First, he draws attention to the fundamental social dimension of domestic life and even of domestic turmoil, not to deny the personal quality of life, but to emphasize the larger circumstances that necessarily help to condition it and to give it meaning. The relations governing the family are clearly subordinated to and made to answer to the larger and more powerful network of relations governing society, to the extent that the coherence and very survival of the family are shown to depend upon the proper alignment of personal and public values.[6] The incest issue, for instance, is not allowed to stand as a purely private crisis that Azo's family alone must somehow face (though the personal pain arising from the situation is clearly present), but rather is presented as a crisis of sweeping social proportions, evidenced in the public trial and punishment of the transgression. While it is true that the burden of the crime falls only on a few individuals, the crime itself is not viewed finally as a violation of family relationships alone, but as a violation of social relations as well.

Second, Byron's portrayal of the family makes a specific political statement by exposing the close connection between family life and public power. One ingredient of Azo's political strength is the family unity that he has created around him, on display for all to see; the secure domestic life that is implied to have been securely in place prior to the incest ordeal reflects the supposedly solid values being disseminated through society under his authority (in much the same way that Werner's family, in Byron's penultimate drama, is taken as a personal sign of the virtues of Werner's political authority).[7] When Hugo and Parisina are caught in their illicit love affair and it becomes clear that everyone except Azo has been in on the secret, the damage is not only emotional but political as well—an insult to and a denial of Azo's authority. This is why he acts swiftly and publicly to punish the offenders. Fully exercising the power at his disposal, he has his own son brutally executed in public and he banishes his wife, replacing them with a new and more submissive family, from which "goodly sons grew by his side" (531), effectively reasserting his authority at the most fundamental level. This is not to question Azo's moral earnestness—when he passes judgment on his wife and son, he doubtless believes he is carrying out the demands of justice (see, for instance, 575–76)—nor to say that the incest affair is handled with such extremity because it poses a direct threat to his position as ruler of the state. Rather, it is to suggest the pervasive quality of political power, which is sustained by its absolute penetration into every facet of human experience, down to the most personal level.

The tale is distinguished further from its predecessors in its treatment of legal procedure. In all of the tales Byron is of course concerned with crime (indeed, this is an abiding interest in much of his later poetry as well),[8] and in *The Corsair* he even addresses the important role of legal relations in dealing with economic crime. But he never describes the legal apparatus actually at work, relying instead on the more exotic (and, perhaps, narratively more interesting) description of the military suppression of criminal activity, which overshadows the significance of legal structures themselves. Here, he subjects his hero fully to the authority of state law, not in such a way as to emphasize every detail of a courtroom proceeding, but in a way that illustrates the broad social function of legal authority, the method by which it exercises this authority, and its direct connection to physical, moral, and religious power.

As one social philosopher has observed recently, in discussing the nature of bourgeois law, "it is in the law that the state's coercive power is most obvious. Yet the law is not presented as an instrument of power."[9] Although the historical setting of the poem is not a bourgeois culture, this insight characterizes very well the spirit in which Byron presents the legal system in *Parisina*. When Azo ascends "his throne of judgment" (135), he does so out of responsibility to society, not out of a self-conscious and blind love of power. Reluctantly he administers the law in order to preserve the values that society holds sacred:

> . . . But yesterday
> I gloried in a wife and son;
> That dream this morning passed away;
> Ere day declines, I shall have none.
> My life must linger on alone;
> Well,—let that pass,—there breathes not one
> Who would not do as I have done.
>
> (198–204)

Even if his actions are sincere and even if they display an obvious and real regard for moral integrity, they are not, however, entirely innocent, for they serve unquestioningly to maintain, at all costs, the prevailing structures of social life, in which Azo has a vested interest. The effect of the legal process, as Azo carries it out, is to "maintain a certain type of . . . individual relations" under state authority.[10] Operating in calculated fashion, with both the physical and ideological instruments of the culture behind it, the law in Azo's hands serves as "the guiding principle of the state";[11] that is, it implements the authority of the state, while hiding ruling interests beneath abstract legal and moral considerations. By assuming absolutely its own rightness, and by deflecting the issue in question entirely away from itself and onto those on trial, the state both demonstrates and at the same time legitimizes its authority.

These two major points of interest (family and law) add significantly to the categories of thought that had dominated the earlier narratives, for they locate the poem's intellectual content clearly *within* the network of governing social relations, hence providing an immediate and approachable basis for examining apparently abstract oppositions. Even while many of the issues and conflicts here are familiar from the earlier tales, the emphasis on the internal processes and mechanisms of social authority is more clearly pronounced. This becomes readily apparent when we consider the way the plot unfolds. There is no catastrophic showdown of the sort that characterizes all of the previous tales, only a brief (if tragic) disruption that is expeditiously dealt with and then programmatically removed from the stage of the public imagination. This focus, which plays down physical conflict, enables us to see the way society implements its own judgments and restraints and carries out its own values without interruption. It gives us a clear picture of social codes at work, one which realistically acknowledges their pervasive and inescapable power, as well as the unflinching exercise of this power by the ruling elite.

One of the major strategical changes that helps this narrative perspective to succeed is in the characterization of the hero. While he displays something of the temperament and sense of injustice that characterize earlier heroes, Hugo is finally unlike his predecessors in that he submits without resistance to controlling codes. Rather than standing moodily outside the culture that has alienated him, banging away stubbornly at its monolithic power structure even while accepting its most deeply rooted values, he is from the first an abiding and loyal (though not weak) citizen and son in every way, except in his love for Parisina, and he never attempts to deny or to escape this fact. Unlike the Giaour, Selim, Lara, and Alp, he never sets as his goal the overthrow of a state leader, attempting instead to overcome his alienation without disturbing the existing power structure. In fact, he fights by his father's side in battle to extend state power:

> It is not that I dread the death—
> For thou has seen me by thy side
> All redly through the battle ride;
> And that not once a useless brand
> Thy slaves have wrested from my hand,
> Hath shed more blood in cause of thine,
> Than e'er can stain the axe of mine.
>
> (234–40)

The authority of a father, the decision of the law, his own subordinate role and final punishment—these are accepted equally as the inescapable facts of his unfortunate situation.

His position towards his world is exemplified clearly in the way he approaches religion, perhaps the most problematic and consistently drawn of all the issues in the tales. When Azo condemns his son to death, he tells him to "address thy prayers to Heaven, / Before its evening stars are met— / Learn if thou there canst be forgiven" (209–11). The unquestioned assumption here of course is that Hugo is wrong, that his situation is beyond discussion, at least in this world, and that only God—if anyone—can forgive him. This scene recalls Francesca's plea to Alp to abandon his sinful ways and pray to God, and also the priest's concerted efforts to bring the Giaour around to religious devotion after a life of crime. The difference is that Hugo does not wrestle with the situation as it is presented to him; in fact, he readily acquiesces in the religious offering. Immediately before his execution he is described "Kneeling at the Friar's knee" (397):

It is a lovely hour as yet
Before the summer sun shall set,
Which rose upon that heavy day,
And mocked it with his steadiest ray;
And his evening beams are shed
Full on Hugo's fated head,
As his last confession pouring
To the monk, his doom deploring
In penitential holiness,
He bends to hear his accents bless
With absolution such as may
Wipe our mortal stains away.

(407–18)

This final scene before Hugo's death powerfully illustrates the extent of Hugo's un-Byronic submission to the controlling institutions of his world. As family, law, and religion rise to the unfortunate occasion, relentlessly exerting their power to preserve social order and individual morality at the expense of individual life, he dutifully defers to each in turn, readily accepting social authority over individuals.

While this characterization marks a radical departure from the formulaic descriptions that had appeared in the earlier tales, it does not undermine the social insights offered in those poems. Rather, it builds upon previous perspectives, developing a more systematic and imaginative analysis of social events. By altering the characterization of the hero, by bringing him more directly into the play of social relations, the tale provides a fuller critique of the actual social conditions that generate social conflict and demand human sacrifice. That is, as with the depictions of the family and of legal procedure, the portrayal of Hugo enables us to approach the conditions of social life from within the framework of dominant relations. Further, the portrayal of Hugo emphasizes the need for individuals to exist within the mainstream of social life; Hugo's submission, in this view, is not a sign of weakness, but an attempt to overcome alienation by participating in and acknowledging the claims of society on him, much as Arnold, in *The Deformed Transformed*, attempts to combat alienation by embodying fully the codes and values of his world.[12]

Hugo's submission, moreover, is not a self-evident indication of the rightness (in either political or moral terms) of the prevailing social network; it is an example of the unavoidable power of this network. His submission, in fact, is accompanied by a compelling negative critique of society, a critique more direct, disturbing, and penetrating than anything Byron had yet written. Without questioning the integrity or the priority of social institutions *per se*, the narrative attacks the particular and deeply rooted values and ideas that undergird those institutions governing the world of the poem, focusing the vital connection between the subjective and objective conditions of social life. So deeply submerged beneath plot-level concerns as to go virtually unnoticed, and cast in such a way as to seem merely a rehash of much that has come before in the tales, this critique nonetheless elucidates deep contradictions between human value and cultural authority in Hugo's world and, further, illustrates the inevitable eruption of these contradictions.

The details of this critique are presented explicitly in Hugo's single, long speech, made after the self-righteous Azo sentences him to die. Here issues ranging from crime to inheritance to women's rights are addressed, unsystematically yet forcefully, and in such a way as to suggest that plot-level events are not transparent. This speech not only stresses the private dimension of Hugo's conflict with his father, pointing out that the son is in reality more sinned against than sinning because his claim on Parisina's affections preceded Azo's; more importantly, it emphasizes that the crisis charted in the tale is really social rather than private in both its origin and consequences. One central matter that illustrates this point is the determination and assignation of criminal conduct. If in the earlier tales a mysterious past crime was a characteristic of Byron's heroes, as though issues of right and wrong were traceable ultimately to an unfathomable and clearly unsettled psychology (for instance, note the Giaour or Conrad), here the nature and fact of the crime are never in question:

> And with the morn he [Azo] sought, and found,
> In many a tale from those around,
> The proof of all he feared to know,
> Their present guilt, his future woe.
> . . . .
> Concealment is no more—they speak
> All circumstance which may compel
> Full credence to the tale they tell.
>
> (120–23, 127–29)

By bringing criminal conduct into full view, Byron shifts the narrative interest away from the mysterious (and often mystifying) allure of the outlaw to the multiple implications of crime. Without denying the authority of the instruments of law, Hugo's speech before his father provides a context for evaluating the dimensions, interests, and presuppositions of this authority. And what becomes clear in the light of his remarks is that the crime of incest exists only because Azo's political power overrides the fundamental human commitment of Hugo and Parisina to one another—Azo's personal claims have state authority behind them; the claims of Parisina and Hugo do not. This difference alone establishes the legal and moral right of Azo to punish the transgressors. This emphasis on the particular conditions surrounding the crime not only suggests the role of social relations in criminal conduct; more importantly, it illustrates that social authority rather than individual conduct is in this case guilty. In the larger context of social life, in fact, the crime tells more about the kind of world that individuals are forced to live in than about personal malice or integrity.

Another way of approaching the crime issue is to consider it in terms of Hugo's personal experience. Because he is a bastard son, he has no way of becoming individually or socially whole, no way of overcoming the alienation and guilt which have accompanied him from birth. As he states it: ". . . my birth and name be base, / And thy [Azo's] nobility of race / Disdained to deck a thing like me" (282–84). His is a "heritage of shame" (245) for reasons not of his making, and yet he is made to bear this shame. Despite his commitment to existing authority, and despite his willing efforts to extend this authority for his father, he can never share it. In fact, any effort on his part to exercise independent judgment or to fulfill basic human needs (as in the case of his affair with Parisina) brings this authority down on him—he can support the codes which govern him, but he cannot question them or act independently of them. Once again, then, the real crime precedes him, traceable first to his father's illicit conduct (as he tells Azo, "thy very crime . . . [was] my birth" [257]) and ultimately to the dominant power structure that allows the willful and arbitrary abuse of human life. What he is—a bastard son—is a reflection of the world into which he is born, evidence of the social crime for which he is personally held responsible.

These social determinants show the narrative conflict in a significantly different light. They not only emphasize that legal procedures are predicated upon specific political interests; they also reveal that even the most fundamental moral questions (in this case, incest) are a product of social relations. Just as the criminal deed described in the poem cannot be viewed as a purely private action, its moral dimension cannot be assessed in terms of purely abstract and universal principles, because these principles are themselves socially mediated and politically charged, made to serve dominant power interests. As Hugo's speech suggests, despite all claims of universal status, values are in fact created by and are inseparable from social reality. Thus, illegality and immorality are demonstrably the same thing, arising from a single network of dominant relations and interests.

A related issue, mentioned above, which helps to clarify the real social dimension of the narrative situation is the shaping power of heritage. In yet another dramatic shift away from the tactics of the earlier tales, Byron here discloses fully the details of the past which impact directly on the present crisis: Azo's lechery and abuse of political power, Hugo's illegitimacy, and Parisina's love for Hugo which preceded her marriage to Azo. The importance of this information, aside from the fact that it shows the crime to be more complex than it might at first appear, is that it at once exposes and challenges ideological assumptions that support political authority. That is, the historical details which show social processes at work and which explain how the incest crime developed contain an inherent denial of the absolutist assumptions behind prevailing power relations.

Moreover, the depiction of the past as knowable helps to clarify why the situation is resolved in the manner that it is. When Hugo describes the full context of his situation, exposing the glaring wrongs that have contributed to the present crime, he is neither simply offering an abstract condemnation of his father, nor attempting to shift the blame from his own shoulders to someone else's; he is explaining how his culture has developed over time, how specific actions and conflicts have contributed to the legitimation of controlling power interests. He is explaining why the legal and public verdict will go against him and the woman who loves him; his "heritage of shame" is at the same time Azo's heritage of social power, and it is built as much upon the back of popular belief as upon military genius and physical daring.

Finally, and perhaps most importantly, Hugo's speech shows that social authority most often discriminates along gender lines. This is suggested most explicitly by the fact that, while Hugo, having been sentenced to death, valiantly addresses his father on the subjects of injustice and inhumanity, Parisina not only remains silent, but also goes through a series of stereotypically feminine responses to extreme pressure: she first weeps (173–82), then faints (348), and then suffers an attack of amnesia (360–85). Like the Byronic heroines who preceded her, she seems to be all beauty and no substance. But, again, while we may fault Byron for such a predictably masculine view of women, we should note as well that within the larger context of the narrative action he offers a compelling defense of Parisina. Her character, after all, is not drawn independently of the oppressive world that has willfully exploited her and, indeed, her pained and confused response to her situation exposes the true horror of patriarchal culture.

For one thing, although Hugo is the spokesperson, and although the central conflict in the narrative is ostensibly between father and son, the point is made forcefully that the real victims from the beginning are women, as power is arbitrarily exercised against them, effectively silencing them and relegating them to the fringes of culture. Hugo's own "heritage of shame," the tale stresses, results from Azo's irresponsible use of his power against a woman. As Hugo angrily puts it:

> Nor are my mother's wrongs forgot,
> Her slighted love and ruined name
>
> .   .   .   .
>
> Her broken heart—my severed head—
> Shall witness for thee from the dead
> How trusty and how tender were
> Thy youthful love—paternal care.

(243–44, 248–51)

Further, Azo's marriage to Parisina is a blatant compromise of a woman who does not care for him. Even if he dotes on her (for instance, see 81–82), it is the dotage on a thing possessed. Despite his affection for her, he never allows her equal (or even human) status. He uses her, for instance, to taunt Hugo (whom she loves) for being illegitimate and powerless (253–63). After Parisina is banished, too, Azo again exercises the privileges of patriarchy, finding "another bride" (530), one who presumably will be loyal and duly submissive.

I am not suggesting here that what Azo lacks is the gift of romantic love. My point, rather, is that with him relations between the sexes are entirely relations of domination. This, in fact, is one of the defining characteristics of the world he rules; the lines of social division are drawn to a large extent according to gender. Hugo's relationship with Parisina, while it is idealized and while Hugo certainly does not demonstrate an entirely humane attitude towards women, challenges the authority of this position by relying on mutual affection and regard rather than upon the arbitrary exercise of power by one person over another. And this, of course, is one reason the relationship is punished with such severity.

Moreover, looking beyond Hugo's speech to the larger context of the narrative, the gender issue is exemplified in the disparity between the title of the poem and the relative obscurity of the title character. In the manner of *The Bride of Abydos*, this poem calls attention to a feminine lead character, only to give her a relatively minor (and entirely passive) role in the story. Every description of and every action by Parisina is stereotypically feminine, proclaiming the beauty and spiritual purity of her gender while assuming her absolute incompetence in the face of public pressure. But, again, this should not be taken as an absolute or reductive position. As Hugo's speech and the general course of the narrative show, Parisina and women in general are allowed *no* entrance into the public world, which is entirely masculine. If Azo's conduct and attitudes can be taken as representative of the ruling social position, then it is clear that Parisina's characterization is as much a product of her world as Azo's is. She is described as weak not because women are weak by nature, but because a patriarchal culture has weakened them. It is this which the title should call attention to; Parisina screams to be heard, even recognized, and yet in a purely masculine world she remains invisible or at best an object to be won or discarded by men.

An additional point on this subject that deserves mention is the distinction that is implicitly drawn in the story between *patriarchy* and *men*. As Juliet Mitchell has observed (in another context), patriarchy does not reduce simply to biology, but rather designates "the relative places of men and women in human history." And, using Freudian vocabulary, she emphasizes that "it is *fathers* not *men* who have the determinate power" in society.[13] This is an important distinction, not only because it casts the gender issue in social rather than biological terms, but also because, in doing so, it suggests that patriarchy oppresses men no less than women. Azo's power, the power of the father is exercised, after all, just as abusively against Hugo as against Parisina. In this view, Hugo cannot be equated with Azo; he is not a representative of patriarchal power, but a victim of it. In fact, his affair with Parisina is presented as a powerful indictment of patriarchy, for it is a human relationship built upon gender equality.

In such a patriarchal world as this, where existing institutions and codes are believed to constitute a fixed and permanent reality, where history is elided and replaced by abstract principles, and where extreme conflict defines everyday life, incest becomes more than a psychological issue. It becomes symbolic, in various ways, of the complex dimensions of the world being portrayed. As we saw above, this particular case of incest is a product of a specific social situation that evolved over time; it is mediated both by personal struggles and injustices (i.e., the father's usurpation of the son in sexual matters) and by public history: the power in Azo's hands is built into and has been passed down by culture itself. Further, as becomes apparent in Hugo's speech, the entire incest issue is to a large extent fabricated; the mother-son attachment is originally an innocent, emotional, mutual commitment made by two individuals to one another, and it becomes incest only when Azo abuses his political power, marrying Parisina to taunt Hugo. The principles and structures of everyday life in the world of the narrative are, historically, isolating and oppressive, as individuals are denied at every turn access to social and thus individual power and rights. Hugo as a bastard son and Parisina as a woman have literally nowhere to turn to satisfy basic human (social) needs; both can serve the state as military or emotional subordinates, but neither can enter into the unalienated stream of social productivity and fulfillment.

That an incestuous affair develops out of this situation not only suggests that the dispossessed often look to their own kind for comfort; it also exemplifies the inescapable need, despite prevailing legal and moral codes, of individuals to be human. Even if the love of Hugo and Parisina for one another is labeled criminal and immoral by social authority, it is in fact an assertion of true morality and a denial of false and abusive ruling principles. As such it exposes the personal and political inhumanity of a world that refuses to question its most basic principles or to measure them in human terms, and claims in the face of all opposition the priority of human freedom.

The incest theme also carries a negative significance, for if Hugo's and Parisina's commitment to one another is an act of defiance on behalf of freedom, at the same time it is the product of a torn world, and as such it bears the imprint of all that is wrong with that world. Their incestuous affair focuses the internal nature of the social oppression they suffer, emphasizing the extent to which experience is interiorized and privatized in their world. They are surrounded by leadership that is divided from the claims and needs of social subordinates (note, for instance, the cold remarks made by Hugo in 234–40, or note Azo's sheer disregard for the rights of his own son), by family life that is shattered by conflicting private interests, and by a system of justice that is divided rigidly from the actual contexts of human experience. Such a world perpetuates itself only by feeding on itself, much as Milton's Sin is tortured and eaten by her own progeny. Even if Hugo and Parisina are in real terms innocent, their commitment to one another cannot promote social or individual strength. It can expose social injustice, but it cannot alleviate it, for it is finally alienated existence, private and self-consuming.

This emphasis on the self-consuming aspect of oppression appears in much of Byron's mature poetry. When he depicts social decay, he rarely maintains that deterioration results from outside forces. In *Marino Faliero, Sardanapalus, Werner, Cain,* and other works he suggests that societies make themselves weak when their relations are predicated upon force, division, and the arbitrary exercise of power, and when their dominant ideas and principles become abstracted from material reality and are made to serve the interests of one group or individual to the exclusion of the larger claims of society itself. While in *Parisina* the incest theme initially may obscure this focus by exploiting our curiosity about a forbidden subject, in fact it represents very compellingly both the fact of social disease and the source of that disease. As Byron handles it, the pressing issue regarding incest is not Hugo's guilt or innocence, but rather the means by which society perpetuates its ruling authority. From the beginning, when we learn of the incestuous affair, Byron sets about establishing the social, historical, and political contexts in which it must be understood; and these contexts expose a culture's self-injustice. Built upon structural and categorical abuses of its own people at both the most public and most private levels, this world is doomed to undermine its own strength and to abuse its own human assets.

One final point bears stressing about the poem—namely, the importance of the narrative structure. The arrangement of the action reflects exactly the intellectual issues at the center of the poem. The story begins with the discovery of a serious moral and social crime and ends with the punishment of that crime and the reestablishment of order. Predictably, Azo at the end of the poem is a sadder but wiser man, one who has suffered greatly in carrying out justice and in assuring that social codes remain in place. At the very center of the tale, however, Hugo's speech exposes the real relations at work beneath surface appearances, describing the objective conditions that have created conflict and shame. His speech calls attention to a current of social life that is ever present in his world, but which is elided by dominant perspectives. The power and pervasiveness of these perspectives are shown in the fact that even his bitterly honest speech cannot change them. The real issues behind social authority are no more acted upon after his speech than before but are quickly suppressed, replaced by Azo's sadness, by his sense of having been wronged, and by his attempts to reinvent a strong family unit. If anything, prevailing codes are strengthened, made to appear as virtually universal truths. And this, we almost forget, is accomplished through the exercise of brute force. Not only is Hugo executed, but Parisina's very existence is absolutely denied public acknowledgment:

No more in palace, hall, or bower,
Was Parisina heard or seen;
Her name—as if she ne'er had been—
Was banished from each lip and ear.

                                                    (503–6)

One important feature of this narrative structure is of course that it enables us to understand the power of prevailing codes. But, more than this, it enables us to measure the apparent situation against actual determining conditions. The linear development of the story as described above supports status quo power relations by rhetorically leading the reader from a situation of order through a moment of crisis and then back to an apparently stable situation. This, however, as we have seen, belies the deep structure of events which at every turn undermines the linear structure and its powerful but false rhetoric of social and moral justice.

Parisina marks a logical end to Byron's Eastern Tales, not simply because it was the last one he wrote before leaving England, but, more importantly, because it collects the issues scattered through the earlier narratives and gives them a more coherent treatment. The tale plays down many of the details that previously had obscured social analysis (Byronic individualism, blind and overly sentimentalized love, stubborn rejection of all social authority) and in fact turns many of these details on their head, reversing the tactics which before had been staples. Here, the past is never in question; the hero's character is readily accessible; the heroine is given a human dimension not seen before (except, perhaps, in the unique case of Gulnare, whose exaggerated masculine conduct makes her very different from Parisina). The consequence is that Byron succeeds in creating a more comprehensive social picture than before. The portrayal of violence, leadership, wealth, the state, religion, and so on is combined successfully with a sophisticated understanding of social values, showing in detail both the power of these values and the willingness of social authority to rely on physical and legal strong-arming when values alone are inadequate to the task of preserving ruling interests.

Further, in describing social deterioration, the tale appears more clearly than its predecessors to be about alienation in general rather than about alienation in particular. That is, in each of the previous tales the main character had stood fixedly in opposition to society, thus encouraging psychological and narrow readings of major issues. Here, the focus is clearly on the alienating effects of prevailing conditions on everyone. Not only are Hugo and Parisina victims of their world; Azo himself (like Giaffir before him) loses everything of importance to him. In replacing the family he has destroyed, he is clearly unhappy; no son can fully replace Hugo (532–33) and no wife, however loyal, can replace Parisina:

He was past all mirth or woe:
Nothing more remained below,

But sleepless nights and heavy days,
A mind all dead to scorn or praise,
A heart which shunned itself—and yet
That would not yield—nor could forget.

(545–50)

Social order is restored, but it is an empty order that provides no fulfillment and no purposeful existence even for those who possess social power. Discord penetrates every level of the culture even while the culture remains standing, showing powerfully the alienation that inevitably accompanies patriarchy.

If the poem lacks the exotic allure of the earlier tales, this is because its imaginative qualities are more intellectual than fanciful. Still, it belongs with this group of poems because it does not so much break new ground as bring a new understanding to the old. Narratively, it is fluid, brief, and precise, suggesting that Byron was now surer of the issues before him. Although he took four years to complete it and although he was never certain of its merit, the tale is a sign that Byron at last had developed a definite intellectual perspective on a range of issues that had occupied him for years and that would continue to occupy him through his years of mature poetry.

8

Conclusion

COLLECTIVELY, the Eastern Tales dramatize powerfully the world into which Byron awoke to find himself famous in 1812. While not every episode can be traced to a specific contemporary event and while not every tyrant is meant to represent the Prince Regent in simple allegorical fashion, still the tales project in a general and yet systematic way a full array of social relations that dominated Byron's world, ranging from religion and the family to war and political leadership. One of the strengths of the tales, in fact, is that they are not reducible to a simple and mechanical blueprint of the period. Self-consciously removed from specific political and social inquiry, they provide a unique and compelling point of entry into culture, allowing us to see it in motion, operating according to given sets of assumptions, exercising its claims of political power, and even deteriorating under the weight of its own internal contradictions.

Not surprisingly, given Byron's failure in Parliament and his growing impatience with the reactionary political scene around him, the tales cast an inexorable pall of gloom, elevating despair to an ostensibly transhistorical, pervasive, and insurmountable fact of human experience. One of the major aims of the present study has been to show that such pessimism is not constitutive but symptomatic, not an accurate portrait of the unchanging human condition but a reflection of human experience as it is lived within specific social frameworks.[1] To historicize the despair issue is to see it as a product of objective, humanly created conditions. From this perspective, even if the characters themselves experience unremitting alienation and even if the narrative voices in the tales project an almost complete lack of hope, this is not because "of the fundamental (and romantic) ironies of man's finite existence,"[2] but rather because alienating and mystifying relations dominate society, crippling human potential. The worlds of the poems are not transparent, nor do the voices in the poems speak independently of social circumstances, offering objective observations about the events being charted. Each narrative voice and each character is implicated in the networks of relations they attempt to describe, challenging its power interests but ultimately sharing its perspectives and values.

This social and historical dimension of despair not only helps to clarify the internal dynamics of the tales by showing us a way past poetic self-representations; it also helps to place Byron more accurately with respect to the other Romantic writers, especially the first-generation poets. In an important respect the despair pervading the tales constitutes an implicit critique of the attitudes that Byron felt dominated the poetry of his older contemporaries. The core issue in this critique is best understood in terms of Byron's quarrel with Wordsworth. As far as Byron was concerned, Wordsworth was a "damned fool" (*BLJ* 5:13), committed to an untenable mysticism and petty nature worship. (As he once angrily and sarcastically said of Wordsworth and his fellow Lake Poets, they "run about their ponds though they cannot fish" [*BLJ* 5:13]; see also *BLJ* 4:324.) While this attitude is doubtless shaded with strong personal animosity,[3] it is also symptomatic of a larger set of problems revolving around the unguarded optimism and apocalyptic fervor that had characterized much of the poetry of the 1790s. Emerging at the exact moment of the French Revolution and its immediate aftermath, the first-generation poets for the most part found it bliss to be alive as they rode the first wave of revolutionary hope and change, and they enthusiastically imagined man's release from all oppressive political authority. Byron, however, maturing at the unfortunate period when the Spirit of the Age that Hazlitt so esteemed was dwindling rapidly and ingloriously into the Spirit of the Regency, saw a world which not only failed to inspire confidence, but which in fact demonstrated forcefully that social reality was more complex and political change more difficult than many had believed just a generation earlier. He saw in a way that his predecessors could not the powerful codes that rule society, the depth and pervasiveness of human injustice, and the insurmountable priority of history. In a world where political reaction was pronounced, the recent past could not be celebrated unabashedly as a period of accomplishment; in a very real sense it weighed like a nightmare on the brain of the living, for its highest ideals had been crushed. Under such conditions, it is understandable that Byron repeatedly emphasized the contradictions of social reality rather than unleashed human freedom, and implied that poets before him simply had misunderstood vital elements in human experience.

The response in the tales to the first-generation Romantics takes the form, most often, of a rejection of crude idealism. For instance, every tale except *The Siege* begins with a celebration of idyllic nature, of a past nobility, or both, only to undermine it by dramatizing the sheer difficulty and oppression of experience. The eulogy to Greece at the beginning of *The Giaour*, for instance, is countered by a narrative in which violence and chaos prevail; the natural beauty that is described at the beginning of *Parisina* is offset by pervasive human atrocity. Even when the characters cling desperately to one ideal or another (as they usually do in their love relationships: note the Giaour's love for Leila, Selim's love for Zuleika, Conrad's love for Medora, Alp's love for Francesca, and Hugo's love for Parisina), their stubborn commitment does not save them and in fact is in most cases directly responsible for despair and slaughter. The tales are explicitly unable to sustain a vision of human peace and fulfillment. They discover, in McGann's words, "that there is no place of refuge, not in desire, not in the mind, not in imagination."[4]

These concerns with social relations and with first-generation Romantic assumptions that appear repeatedly in the tales subsequently evolve into a fairly sophisticated and systematic poetic vision grounded upon a commitment to understanding the dominant structures of social and historical process. This is not to say that Byron ever escaped the problematic within which Romanticism developed (idealist and retrogressive tendencies in the tales and in the later poetry are quite pronounced), but rather that he found a way to articulate aspects of the Romantic dilemma that are but sketchily drawn by other writers of the period. His poetry written after his departure from England begins for the most part from the positions arrived at in the tales and expands them into an increasingly astute and imaginative analysis of society, though more often than not his views continue to be cast in vague and emotionally charged language that obscures active social interests.

Even in *The Island,* for example, Byron's last narrative tale and a poem that at first glance appears to be a descent from the satirical heights of social commentary in *Don Juan* to the self-indulgent valleys of earlier writings, he continued exploring the codes, structures, and relations of social reality.[5] In this admittedly bizarre retelling of the mutiny on *The Bounty* he imaginatively recreates William Bligh's story in such a way as to highlight opposite ways of regarding society, and he dramatizes the superiority of one perspective over the other. In Christian he resurrects the Byronic hero of the Eastern Tales in order to show the destructive capacity once again of crude individualistic assumptions. Drawn almost entirely in terms of sheer ego, Christian is set rigidly against all human exchange:

> Stern, and aloof a little from the rest,
> Stood Christian, with his arms across his chest.
> The ruddy, reckless, dauntless hue once spread
> Along his cheek was livid now as lead;
> His light-brown locks, so graceful in their flow,
> Now rose like startled vipers o'er his brow.
> Still as a statue, with his lips comprest
> To stifle even the breath within his breast,
> Fast by the rock, all menacing, but mute,
> He stood; and, save a slight beat of his foot,
> Which deepen'd now and then the sandy dint
> Beneath his heel, his form seem'd turn'd to flint.
>
> (3. 85–96)

As the tale illustrates, such egoism and individualism are signs of extreme alienation, of the utter privatization of human experience. Moreover, they are signs of inevitable social deterioration, not only because they reflect a world where the avenues of human investment have been oppressively narrowed, setting individuals viciously against one another, but also because (relatedly) they obscure the larger power relations that rule society and that have created an ominous situation. All this is presented directly, as Byron refuses to idealize Christian's blind resistance, and in fact confidently and firmly condemns the mindset with which Christian is identified, asserting unflinchingly its dangerous potential. Compared with earlier Byronic heroes such as Conrad, Christian does not appear to be strong and moral, but simply wrong.

While assigning Christian to violent death, Byron allows his counterpart, Torquil, to live and even celebrates his survival. Unlike Christian, Torquil is not "of a higher order" (3. 139), and this is precisely what Byron celebrates in his character. A rebel who wants to create a better world, Torquil does not insist on utopian bliss where all the hardships of life are eliminated; he insists rather on the freedom to participate in society and to challenge it if it fails to meet basic human needs. Further, he openly embraces the community of which he is a part, accepting struggle as a constituent part of social existence and working to create a situation where destructive struggle is minimized. While Byron's handling is perhaps too simplistic, or at least heavy-handed, it states emphatically that *human* survival comes from *social* commitment:

> Again their own shore rises on the view,
> No more polluted with a hostile hue;
> No sullen ship lay bristling o'er the foam,
> A floating dungeon:—all was hope and home!
> A thousand proas darted o'er the bay,
> With sounding shells, and heralded their way;
> The chiefs came down, around the people pour'd,
> And welcomed Torquil as a son restored;
> The women throng'd, embracing and embraced
> By Neuha, asking where they had been chased,
> And how escaped? The tale was told; and then
> One acclamation rent the sky again;
> And from that hour a new tradition gave
> Their sanctuary the name of "Neuha's Cave."
> A hundred fires, far flickering from the height,
> Blazed o'er the general revel of the night,
> The feast in honour of the guest, return'd
> To peace and pleasure, perilously earn'd;
> As only the yet infant world displays.
>
> (4. 401–20)

The understanding of social struggle and the discriminations of social attitudes and ideologies present in this poem emphasize strongly the perspective that dominates the general body of Byron's work, demonstrating a mind in "permanent dialogue"[6] with the world. Even the dramas, which (after the tales) appear to be the least sophisticated of his poems, are powerful in this respect, and in some ways they are among his best work because they actively expose the *internal* mechanisms of society, both material and ideological and, moreover, because they find a way to document large and usually nebulous structures of social thought. Ranging widely over a variety of concerns, from the state and law to religion and art, the dramas offer a comprehensive portrait of the systemic quality of all personal and social life, emphasizing specifically the relations between the ideas governing culture and actual social conditions. And with increasing conviction, the dramas illustrate how ideals and values that ignore historical process and basic human needs imperil culture.[7] The historical trag-edies (*Marino Faliero, Sardanapalus, The Two Foscari*), the metaphysical dramas (*Manfred, Cain, Heaven and Earth*), and the final personal tragedies (*Werner* and *The Deformed Transformed*) are all variations on this theme, portrayals of human crisis as social crisis. Even *Manfred*, the most abstract and individualistic of the dramas, is grounded solidly in a social problematic, revealing the absolute claim of history on individuals. Manfred's proud defiance of authority and his power to command spirits, while valiant assertions of human strength, are in a real sense expressions of his desperate need to control his destiny in a world that has entirely isolated him. Overwhelmed by mystifying and alienating circumstances, he is thrown back entirely upon sheer private ego, which he cultivates to no avail. He cannot establish a contextless present of untrammeled and un-challenged individual power, and, finally, he cannot even survive in isolation. At every turn, his actions are claims to freedom and strength under the very conditions of their denial.

Byron once remarked to Moore: "I think it [society] *fatal* to all original undertakings of every kind" (*BLJ* 9:119). This comment might be taken as a key to Byron's intellectual perspective and poetic interest. He wanted to understand both *why* society was constituted in such a way that it consistently worked against humanity's best interest, and *what kinds* of changes would be required to rectify the situation. To this end he worked imaginatively and often hurriedly, creating an astonishing variety of world-pictures taken from such diverse sources as ancient Greece, feudal culture, the Near East, Russia, Europe, and England. And in every instance the poetic impulse was the same, drawing its vigor from the common power relations defining social reality.

While we need not claim that Byron self-consciously directed his career towards creating a political poetry (though such a position definitely is arguable, especially with respect to the poetry written after about 1820),[8] we should nevertheless recognize this powerful social dimension of his poetic vision, present even in his earliest writings. From the beginning, his work displays a compelling interest in the deep structures of society, and, despite the pessimism that frequently characterizes its poetic voice, it constitutes a praxis that is fundamentally hopeful, if only because it is doggedly committed to exposing social contradictions and injustices. His poems enable us to understand more fully the ideological and political dimensions of social reality, and thus they teach us a plausible and coherent way of approaching them. If we must fault the tales or his other poems for their excessive emotionalism and for their frequent self-indulgence, we must also commend them for contributing significantly to our understanding not only of Byron's world, but also of our own.

Notes

Chapter 1. Toward a Context for Studying Byron's Eastern Tales

1. Byron refers to this poem as "Porson's 'Devil's Walk.'" For the confusion surrounding Byron's reference see *BLJ* 3:240, note 2. For a brief and insightful commentary on Byron's "The Devil's Drive" see Carl Woodring, *Politics in English Romantic Poetry* (Cambridge: Harvard University Press, 1970), 172.

2. To cite only two examples, note Robert F. Gleckner's reference to *Werner* as "melodramatic claptrap," in *Byron and the Ruins of Paradise* (Baltimore: The Johns Hopkins University Press, 1967), 318n, and Samuel C. Chew's remark in his preface to *The Dramas of Lord Byron: A Critical Study* (1915; reprint ed., New York: Russell & Russell, 1964) that *Werner* "is about as complete a failure as anything in literature."

3. Jerome J. McGann, *The Romantic Ideology: A Critical Investigation* (Chicago and London: University of Chicago Press, 1983), 1.

4. For an account of the specific personal pressures Byron was operating under during these years, see Leslie A. Marchand, *Byron: A Biography*, 3 vols. (New York: Alfred A. Knopf, 1957), especially pp. 327–607. See also David V. Erdman's scrupulously researched essays, "Lord Byron and the Genteel Reformers," *PMLA* 56 (1941): 1065–94; "Lord Byron as Rinaldo," *PMLA* 57 (1942): 189–231; "Byron and Revolt in England," *Science and Society* 11 (1947): 234–48; and "Byron and 'the New Force of the People,'" *Keats-Shelley Journal* 11 (1962): 47–64. See also Woodring, *Politics in English Romantic Poetry*, 149–229; Peter J. Manning, "Tales and Politics: *The Corsair, Lara,* and *The White Doe of Rylstone,*" in *Byron: Poetry and Politics: Seventh International Byron Symposium, Salzburg 1980,* ed. James Hogg (Salzburg, Austria: Institut für Anglistik & Amerikanistik, Universität Salzburg, 1981), 204–30; and Jerome J. McGann, *"Don Juan" in Context* (New York and London: University of Chicago Press), 11–34.

5. Byron of course was always capable of statements that contradict this one, as in his remark to Caroline Lamb, only a few months after the letter to Harness, that ". . . we are *all* selfish, nature did that for us" (*BLJ* 2:170). But his general position (and his hope) seem to have been that humanity is not instinctively malicious.

6. Catherine Belsey, *Critical Practice* (London and New York: Methuen, 1980), 122.

7. McGann, *The Romantic Ideology,* 145.

8. I am not arguing here that Byron's thought was as careful and consistent as that of Blake, Wordsworth, and Shelley in their respective intellectual and poetic efforts. I merely wish to suggest that his position, even during these highly emotional and taxing years, is not quite as incoherent as might at first appear and that in fact there is a definable point of view both in his letters and in his verse.

9. See, for instance, *BLJ* 3:219 and 42; *BLJ* 4:326; *BLJ* 9:14; and the "Addition to the Preface" to *Childe Harold's Pilgrimage* 1–2.

10. See Thomas Moore, *Letters and Journals of Lord Byron: with Notices of His Life* (London, 1830), 2:82–84.

11. John Locke, *Two Treatises of Government*, ed., Peter Laslett (Cambridge: Cambridge University Press, 1960), 300.

12. Jean-Jacques Rousseau, *"On the Social Contract," with "Geneva Manuscript" and "Political Economy,"* ed. Roger D. Masters, trans. Judith R. Masters (New York: St. Martin's Press, 1978), 52–53.

13. Rousseau, *On the Social Contract*, 52–53.

14. Rousseau, *On the Social Contract*, 53.

15. In this view, the theories of Locke and Rousseau are simply palatable Hobbesianism. For an excellent discussion of the common ties between Hobbes and Locke, see C. B. Macpherson, *The Political Theory of Possessive Individualism: Hobbes to Locke* (Oxford: The Clarendon Press, 1962), especially pages 91–92, 106, and 219–20. Also, for helpful insights into social contract theory, see Jurgen Habermas, *Theory and Practice*, trans. John Viertel (Boston: Beacon Press, 1973), 97–101, and *Communication and the Evolution of Society*, trans. Thomas McCarthy (Boston: Beacon Press, 1979), 185–86. Finally, for a recent discussion of the relationship between individual and society, see Roy Bhaskar, "On the Possibility of Social Scientific Knowledge and the Limits of Naturalism" in vol. 3 of *Issues in Marxist Philosophy*, eds. John Mepham and David-Hillel Ruben (Sussex, Eng.: The Harvester Press, 1979).

16. For a contemporary view of society more in line with the social contract thinkers, see Shelley's *Declaration of Rights*, in Roger Ingpen and Walter E. Peck, eds., *The Complete Works of Percy Bysshe Shelley* (London and New York: The Julian Editions, 1928) 5:271: "Government has no rights; it is a delegation from several individuals for the purpose of securing their own. It is therefore just, only so far as it exists by their consent, useful only so far as it operates to their well-being." This of course is an early work (1812), much influenced by Paine, and Shelley's thinking matures decidedly by the time he writes *A Philosophical View of Reform*, but it indicates a common attitude at the time Byron was writing the tales.

17. Shelley, *Declaration of Rights*, 5:274.

18. Ernest Hartley Coleridge, ed., *Coleridge: Poetical Works* (1912; reprint ed., London and New York: Oxford University Press, 1973).

19. Ernest de Selincourt, ed., *The Prelude; or, Growth of a Poet's Mind* (Oxford: The Clarendon Press, 1959).

20. For a discussion of the retrogressive social views of such writers as Cobbett and Ruskin, see Raymond Williams, *Culture and Society, 1780–1950* (1958; reprint ed., New York and London: Harper Torchbooks, 1966), 12–20 and 130–48.

21. George Rudé, *Revolutionary Europe: 1783–1815* (1964; reprint ed., New York: Harper Colophon Books, 1975), 263.

22. I am relying here on E. J. Hobsbawm, *The Age of Revolution: 1789–1848* (New York: New American Library, 1962), 109, 116.

23. Quoted in A. L. Morton, *A People's History of England* (1938; reprint ed., New York: International Publishers, 1974), 353.

24. For a detailed discussion of this subject by a Romantic writer, see Shelley's *A Philosophical View of Reform*, in Ingpen and Peck, 7:5–55.

25. Morton, *A People's History of England*, 361.

26. Hobsbawm, *The Age of Revolution*, 117.

27. John Kinnaird, *William Hazlitt: Critic of Power* (New York: Columbia University Press, 1978), 83–84.

28. I am here relying almost entirely on Harvey's book (New York: St. Martin's Press, 1978), 59–63. Subsequent references to this book will be cited parenthetically in the text. For an additional excellent social history of the period that has been influential here, see E. P. Thompson, *The Making of the English Working Class* (1963; reprint ed., New York: Vintage Books, 1966), 451–710.

29. As Harvey puts it, "By lending themselves to a political campaign against the class to which they belonged, they [the reformers] effectively channelled off much popular energy which, if denied a parliamentary outlet, might have manifested itself in a much more dangerous extra-parliamentary organization" (*Britain in the Early Nineteenth Century*, 225).

30. For a discussion of Byron's Rochdale affairs, see Erdman's "Lord Byron," in *Romantic Rebels*, 173–74. See also *BLJ* 2:114–15, 127, and 203.

31. Note, for instance, Byron's satirical ballad on Hobhouse in 1820. This funny but ultimately very serious poem appears in *Poetry 7*, pp. 66–69, and its political content has been discussed by David Erdman in "Byron and 'the New Force of the People,'" 57ff.

32. Byron's parliamentary involvement has been studied most fully and most helpfully by David Erdman. See his *PMLA* articles (note 4, above) and his essays in *Romantic Rebels*, 161–227.

33. See, for instance, Leslie Marchand's record of Byron's relationship with Dr. James Kennedy, in *Byron: A Biography*, 3:1104–5.

34. G. Wilson Knight, *Lord Byron: Christian Virtues* (London: Routledge & Kegan Paul, 1952), 19.

Chapter 2. *The Giaour*

1. Byron's indebtedness to Eastern lore is well documented and is not a part of the present study. It is worth noting, however, that Edward W. Said's study of the historical (as opposed to the purely literary) significance of the Orient to the European mind is particularly useful to the serious reader of Byron's tales, because it documents the far-reaching social and political determinants beneath the purely literary interest and the exterior exoticism which Byron exploits. Further, while Said is not concerned directly with Byron's poetry, he does note that Byron "had a political vision of the Near Orient," a fact which, I will argue, is illustrated repeatedly in the tales. See *Orientalism* (1978; reprint ed., New York: Vintage Books, 1979), especially p. 192. For discussions of the East that are relevant to Byron's tales, see Martha Pike Conant, *The Oriental Tale in England in the Eighteenth Century* (New York: Columbia University Press, 1908); Samuel C. Chew, *The Crescent and the Rose: Islam and England during the Renaissance* (1937; reprint ed., New York: Octagon Books, Inc., 1965); and Wallace Cable Brown, "Byron and English Interest in the Near East," *Studies in Philology* 34 (1937): 56–64.

2. This is of course not to suggest that literary and biographical sources are not to be trusted as guides for informed critical analysis of *The Giaour*. Several studies make excellent use of these sources. See, for instance, Peter J. Manning, *Byron and His Fictions* (Detroit: Wayne State University Press, 1978), 35–39, and Peter L. Thorslev, Jr., *The Byronic Hero: Types and Prototypes* (Minneapolis: University of Minnesota Press, 1962), 146–53.

3. George Finlay, *A History of Greece from its Conquest by the Romans to the Present Time: B.C. 146 to A.D. 1864* (1877; reprint ed., New York: AMS Press, Inc., 1970), 5:264.

4. On this issue, Finlay says of Hassan Ghazi's excursion into the Morea that "Hassan hunted down their [the Arnauts'] dispersed bands over the peninsula, and exterminated them without mercy. The heads of the chieftains were sent to Constantinople, and exposed before the gate of the serai, while a pyramid was formed of those of the soldiers under the walls of Tripolitza" (*A History of Greece*, 5:264–65).

5. Raymond Williams, *The Country and the City* (Oxford: Oxford University Press, 1973), passim; see also Williams's *Problems in Materialism and Culture* (London: New Left Books, 1980), 67–85.

6. For a helpful discussion of the concept of human nature along the lines suggested here, see Antonio Gramsci, *Selections from the Prison Notebooks*, trans. and ed. Quintin Hoare and Geoffrey Nowell Smith (New York: International Publishers, 1971), 351–57.

7. Karl Marx, *Grundrisse: Foundations of the Critique of Political Economy*, trans. Martin Nicolaus (New York: Vintage Books, 1973), 156.

8. M. I. Finley, "Utopianism Ancient and Modern," in *The Critical Spirit: Essays in Honor of Herbert Marcuse*, eds. Kurt H. Wolff and Barrington Moore, Jr. (Boston: Beacon Press, 1968), 6.

9. For a study of the connection between Byron and the Brontës, see Winifred Gerin, "Byron's Influence on the Brontës," *Keats-Shelley Memorial Bulletin* 17 (1966): 1–19. See also Andrew Rutherford, *Byron: A Critical Study* (Stanford, Calif.: Stanford University Press, 1961), 41–44.

10. This is not to say that other classes never use violence, or to suggest that the crimes described in the poem are not in the *first* instance crimes of passion. It is simply to stress that, ultimately, even the most personal acts are socially grounded.

11. William H. Marshall, "The Accretive Structure of Byron's 'The Giaour,'" *Modern Language Notes* 76 (1961): 509.

12. Karl Marx, *Capital: A Critique of Political Economy*, trans. Samuel Moore and Edward Aveling, ed. Frederick Engels (1887; reprint ed., Moscow: Progress Publishers, 1954), 83.

13. Karl Marx and Frederick Engels, *The German Ideology* (1964; reprint ed., Moscow: Progress Publishers, 1976), 51.

14. Again, see Erdman's essays in *PMLA* 56 (1941): 1065–94, and 57 (1942): 189–231.

15. Marshall, "The Accretive Structure of Byron's 'The Giaour,'" 502.

16. The social and historical focus which the accretions provide makes *The Giaour* a fundamentally different kind of poem from, say, Rogers's *The Voyage of Columbus*, probably the model for Byron's narrative technique. It is true that Rogers wanted to offer a historical perspective in his poem and noted in his preface that *The Voyage*, in presenting the adventures and trials of Columbus, was "full of historical allusions." But Rogers's poetic vision is largely uncritical and given more to sensationalism and nostalgia than to serious historical inquiry. From the beginning, for example, he assumes that his protagonist "was a person of extraordinary virtue and piety, acting, as he conceived under the sense of a divine impulse," and he sets out to portray Columbus's voyage from this limited point of view, as a triumph of virtue and perseverance. Thus, despite the use of fragments (really contrived shifts and turns which are meant to provide the story with an air of authenticity) and despite the historical interest, the narrative is highly conventional and predictable; the Christian position described in the Preface and in the introductory lines of the poem is momentarily confronted by evil spirits, and Columbus at one point faces a possible mutiny, but the forces of good are never really threatened or shown in anything other than a positive light, and in the end Columbus in a vision is given to understand the greatness of his accomplishment. Rogers never challenges his hero and, more to the point, never examines the underlying assumptions which give events their particular flavor and importance. The motives in the poem are evident and easily assessed, as are the obstacles; there are no nebulous or hidden issues exposed through the narrative. Thus, while *The Voyage* serves as a model, it is not entirely a satisfactory model. Byron does not simply take over its form and content, but rather modifies both radically so that his historical perspective is to a greater extent historically grounded, attuned more clearly to the pressures, the flux, and the interpenetrating elements which inform and enliven material existence. Accordingly, Byron's fragments, more than Rogers's, suggest actual turns of thought, abrupt shifts of attitude and levels of insight—in short, the pressures of history and society. This is not meant to denigrate

Rogers—we should recall, after all, that Byron dedicated *The Giaour* to him—but rather to suggest the way and to what extent Byron was able to build upon an important poetic source.

17. Peter B. Wilson, "'Galvinism upon Mutton': Byron's Conjuring Trick in *The Giaour*," *Keats-Shelley Journal* 24 (1975): 126.

18. Gleckner, *Byron and the Ruins of Paradise*, 99.

Chapter 3. *The Bride of Abydos*

1. Leslie A. Marchand, *Byron: A Portrait* (Chicago: The University of Chicago Press, 1970), 148, 155.

2. On this subject, see Marchand, *Byron's Poetry: A Critical Introduction* (Cambridge: Harvard University Press, 1965), 63.

3. For a discussion of Byron's relationship to his reading public at this time, see Philip W. Martin, *Byron: A Poet before His Public* (Cambridge: Cambridge University Press, 1982), 30–63.

4. For a helpful discussion of the openings of all the tales see Gleckner, *Byron and the Ruins of Paradise*, 91–190 passim.

5. See the "Introduction" to *Romanticism*, ed. John B. Halsted (New York: Harper & Row, 1969), 13.

6. For a full interpretation of *The Rime* along these lines, see Edward E. Bosetetter, *The Romantic Ventriloquists: Wordsworth, Coleridge, Keats, Shelley, Byron* (Seattle and London: University of Washington Press, 1963), 109–18.

7. See, for example, Robert Penn Warren's introductory essay to his edition of *The Rime of the Ancient Mariner* (New York: Reynal and Hitchcock, 1946). Or see the introductory comments on the poem in Marius Bewley, ed., *The English Romantic Poets: An Anthology* (New York: The Modern Library, 1970), 336–38.

8. See, for example, Charles E. Robinson, *Shelley and Byron: The Snake and Eagle Wreathed in Fight* (Baltimore: The Johns Hopkins University Press, 1976), 17–40.

9. Geoffrey H. Hartman, *Wordsworth's Poetry, 1787–1814* (New Haven and London: Yale University Press, 1964), 42.

10. A statement by Marx in the *Economic and Philosophic Manuscripts of 1844* throws light on this matter: "But *nature* too, taken abstractly, for itself—nature fixed in isolation from man—is *nothing* for man. It goes without saying that the abstract thinker who has committed himself to intuiting, intuits nature abstractly. Just as nature lay enclosed in the thinker in the form of the absolute idea, in the form of a thought-entity—in a shape which was obscure and enigmatic even to him—so by letting it emerge from himself he has really let emerge only this *abstract nature*, only nature as a *thought-entity*." Quoted in *Karl Marx and Frederick Engels: Collected Works* (New York: International Publishers, 1975), 3:345.

11. For a discussion of this idea as it appears in *Werner*, see Daniel P. Watkins, "Byron and the Poetics of Revolution," *The Keats-Shelley Journal* 34 (1985): 95–130.

12. The most fundamental elements in the social nexus, tightly and firmly layered beneath conscious practice and thought, are class-defined and class-dominated, and Giaffir, as ruler of the state, finds his power in this social fact. As Raymond Williams states (writing in a different context): "What is decisive is not only the conscious system of ideas and beliefs, but the whole lived process as practically organized by specific meanings and values." And, as Marx explains, these meanings and values are always organized around ruling-class power. See Williams, *Marxism and Literature* (Oxford: Oxford University Press, 1977), 109. Note also Marx's famous statement that "the ideas of the ruling class are in every epoch the ruling ideas" and his subsequent discussion of the production of consciousness in *The German Ideology*, 67–71.

13. Daniel P. Deneau, *Byron's Narrative Poems of 1813: Two Essays* (Salzburg, Austria: Institut für Englische Sprache und Literatur, Universität Salzburg, 1975), 45. See also Jennie Calder, "The Hero as Lover: Byron and Women," in *Byron: Wrath and Rhyme*, ed. Alan Bold (London: Vision Press Limited; Totowa, NJ: Barnes & Noble Books, 1983), 103–24.

14. I am relying here on the general comments by Terry Eagleton in *Literary Theory: An Introduction* (Minneapolis: University of Minnesota Press, 1983), 18–22.

Chapter 4. *The Corsair*

1. For a full account of the publication of *The Corsair* volume, see McGann's commentary in *BCPW* 3:444–45; see also Manning's "Tales and Politics," 204–19.

2. See also McGann's *"Don Juan" in Context*, 20.

3. John Charles Leonard Simonde de Sismondi, *A History of the Italian Republics; Being a View of the Rise, Progress, and Fall of Italian Freedom* (New York: Harper & Brothers, 1864), 94.

4. Sismondi, *History of the Italian Republics*, 44–45.

5. See, for instance, Marchand, *Byron's Poetry*, 64–66, and Karl Kroeber, *Romantic Narrative Art* (Madison: The University of Wisconsin Press, 1960), 142.

6. Marx, *Economic and Philosophic Manuscripts of 1844*, 3:299.

7. Russell Jacoby, *Social Amnesia: A Critique of Conformist Psychology from Adler to Laing* (Boston: Beacon Press, 1975), 104.

8. Marx and Engels, *The German Ideology*, 79, 75, 80. On the historical development of merchant capital, see also Christopher Hill, *The Century of Revolution: 1603–1714* (1961; reprint ed., New York: W. W. Norton & Company, 1966), passim.

9. Gramsci, *Selections from the Prison Notebooks*, 195–96.

10. Karl Marx, *A Contribution to the Critique of Political Economy*, trans. S. W. Ryazanskaya, ed. Maurice Dobb (Moscow: Progress Publishers, 1970), 20.

11. Marx and Engels, *The German Ideology*, 349.

12. Thorslev, *The Byronic Hero*, 65–83 and 146–64.

13. E. J. Hobsbawm, *Primitive Rebels: Studies in Archaic Forms of Social Movement in the 19th and 20th Centuries* (New York: W. W. Norton & Company, 1959), 23.

14. E. J. Hobsbawm, *Bandits* (New York: Pantheon, 1981), 26.

15. Williams, *Culture and Society*, 140.

16. Hobsbawm, *Bandits*, 41–57.

17. Marx's comment about love relationships voices this point clearly: "This relationship . . . reveals the extent to which man's *need* has become *human* need; the extent to which, therefore, the *other* person as a person has become for him a need—the extent to which he in his individual existence is at the same time a social being." See *Economic and Philosophic Manuscripts of 1844*, 3:296.

18. Erdman, "Byron and the 'New Force of the People,'" 54.

19. Fredric Jameson, *The Political Unconscious: Narrative as a Socially Symbolic Act* (Ithaca: Cornell University Press, 1981), 102.

20. Jacoby, *Social Amnesia*, 113.

21. For a discussion of Byron's idealization of women, see Gloria T. Hull, "The Byronic Heroine and Byron's *The Corsair*," *Ariel* 9 (1978): 71–83; Jennie Calder, "The Hero as Lover: Byron and Women," 103–24; Joanna E. Rapf, "The Byronic Heroine: Incest and the Creative Process," *Studies in English Literature* 21 (1981): 637–45; and especially the excellent essay by Marina Vitale, "The Domesticated Heroine in Byron's *Corsair* and William Hone's Prose Adaptation," *Literature & History* 10 (1984): 72–94.

22. Hopeful, at least, in that it was committed to certain traditional values, and in that it expressed a utopian impulse.

23. See Jameson, *The Political Unconscious,* 102.

24. Jameson, *The Political Unconscious,* 102.

Chapter 5. *Lara*

1. Karl Kroeber, *Romantic Narrative Art,* 142.

2. McGann, *"Don Juan" in Context,* 20.

3. L. Leontyev, *Political Economy: A Condensed Course* (New York: International Publishers, 1974), 27. A fuller and perhaps more reliable study of this aspect of feudalism can be found in Perry Anderson, *Passages from Antiquity to Feudalism* (London: New Left Books, 1974), 147–53.

4. Quoted in *A Dictionary of Marxist Thought,* ed. Tom Bottomore (Cambridge: Harvard University Press, 1983), 170.

5. A. L. Morton, *A People's History of England,* 53.

6. For an excellent, lucid discussion of the role consent plays in social domination, see Raymond Williams's chapter on "hegemony" in *Marxism and Literature,* 108–14.

7. *A Dictionary of Marxist Thought,* 170.

8. Georg Lukács, *Realism in Our Time: Literature and the Class Struggle,* trans. John and Necke Mander (New York: Harper & Row, 1967), 21.

9. Helpful comments on the social, political, and historical dimensions of language, relevant to the discussion here, appear in Antonio Gramsci, *Selections from the Prison Notebooks,* 324–25 and 349, and in Noam Chomsky, *Language and Responsibility: Based on Conversations with Mitsou Ronat,* trans. John Viertel (New York: Pantheon Books, 1977), 191.

10. Williams, *Marxism and Literature,* 115–16.

11. Williams, *The Sociology of Culture,* 187.

12. Williams, *The Sociology of Culture,* 187.

13. For conventional psychological interpretations of this characterization, see Anahid Melikian, *Byron and the East* (Beirut: American University of Beirut, 1977), 67, and Marchand, *Byron's Poetry,* 67.

14. For a discussion of the personal and political dimensions of the uprising in *Marino Faliero,* see Daniel P. Watkins, "Violence, Class Consciousness, and Ideology in Byron's History Plays," *ELH* 48 (1981): 799–816.

15. Carl Lefevre, "Lord Byron's Fiery Convert of Revenge," *Studies in Philology* 49 (1952): 475.

16. See, for instance, William H. Marshall, *The Structure of Byron's Major Poems* (Philadelphia: University of Pennsylvania Press, 1962), 50–62.

17. Note, for instance, his confused portrayal of women in *The Deformed Transformed,* a play which he literally breaks off when his heroine begins to take on a major role.

Chapter 6. *The Siege of Corinth*

1. For a full discussion of the tale's compositional history, see McGann's commentary in *BCPW* 3:479–81.

2. Note for instance the remarks by William J. Calvert, *Byron: Romantic Paradox* (1935; reprint ed., New York: Russell & Russell, 1962), 116; Gleckner, *Byron and the Ruins of Paradise,* 164; and Marchand, *Byron's Poetry,* 68.

3. For a discussion of how historical context affects Byron's expository strategies and accomplishments, see Kroeber, *Romantic Narrative Art,* 144–45.

4. It is worth noting here Byron's contempt for Lord Elgin, Payne Knight, and the

other so-called "antiquarians" of the period, whose notions of history were popular and, as far as Byron was concerned, clearly unsatisfactory. He doubtless wanted to avoid the simplification and questionable motives of these men and yet saw no clear alternative path to take. (For an instance of his feelings toward the antiquarians, see *Childe Harold's Pilgrimage* 2. 11–15, or *The Age of Bronze*.)

5. While the advertisement gives an air of historical authenticity and indeed establishes the poem's historical perspective, it should not be taken as a sign that Byron had researched his subject fully. His narrative adheres only loosely to the details of the advertisement, adopting the general setting and situation that it describes, while creating its own version of the situation.

6. George Finlay, *A History of Greece from its Conquest by the Romans to the Present Time*, 5:220.

7. The impressions of Gifford and Murray are noted in McGann, *BCPW* 3:480–81. Contemporary reviews of the poem are compiled in Donald H. Reiman, ed., *The Romantics Reviewed: Contemporary Reviews of British Romantic Writers. Part B: Byron and Regency Society Poets*, 5 vols. (New York and London: Garland Publishing, 1972).

8. In his new edition of *The Siege*, McGann has removed forty-five lines which, since the 1832 edition, have served as the opening section to the poem, on the grounds that these lines never appeared with the poem until after Byron's death. It should be noted that, while McGann is right to restore the poem to its original form, these lines are relevant to *The Siege* (see *BLJ* 4:337 and *n*), serving much the same function as the introductory sections to the other tales. Most importantly, these "Lines Associated with *The Siege*" identify some of the categories of social thought that provide a basis for evaluating the ensuing narrative action. Like the introductions to *The Giaour* and *The Bride*, these lines are laden with nostalgia and longing for a noble past; but, in condensing and sharpening his sentiments, Byron offers a more plausible social ideal than before— not an obvious fantasy, but a credible picture of how people, under different circumstances, might live—presenting human sensibilities realistically, yet in the fullness of their strength. In describing his 1810 travels to the East, he notes in passing of the company he kept:

> . . . we had health, and we had hope,
> Toil and travel, but no sorrow.
> We were of all tongues and creeds;—
> Some were those who counted beads,
> Some of mosque, and some of church,
> And some, or I mis-say, of neither;
> Yet through the wide world might ye search,
> Nor find a motlier crew nor blither.
>
> (16–23)

While this scene is unabashedly hopeful, it is not naively idealistic; it constitutes a viable model of human relations against which other social activities can be measured. The scene acknowledges individual and even social *difference*, imagining it as a strengthening human characteristic; the social life that is celebrated here benefits from the differences of language, culture, and religion, finding the variety of the world in both its natural and social forms bearable and even inspiring. The story told in *The Siege* does not so much trace the decline of this solidarity as describe conditions and attitudes which prevent it. The narrative is, as it were, a reverse image of this scene, a direct contradiction of its optimism and social perspective. Rather than presenting a world in which different value systems can coexist and contribute to a single goal of human strength and betterment, the events of the story describe how the constituent elements of a society can turn on one another in Urizenic fashion, producing (despite professions of high principle and good intentions) a fragmented, privatized, and doom-ridden reality.

9. I am taking this phrase from Paul M. Sweezy's book by the same title, *The Present as History: Essays and Reviews on Capitalism and Socialism* (New York: Monthly Review Press, 1953).

10. This is not to say that social change, as the tale presents it, is reducible ultimately to shifting perspectives, as though consciousness or ideas alone determine social process. One effect of the historical framework of the poem, as noted above, is to preclude such idealization. The real struggle between the Turks and the Venetians for control of the Morea is firmly set at the center of the narrative as an insurmountable fact of reality, subsuming all other issues. But Byron shows at the same time that such political struggles as this are always accompanied by the intellectual and moral positions that are not simply passive reflections, but active, shaping forces—powerful weapons within any political situation—and his major focus is on the power of ideology over the relations and material processes of social life.

11. This phrase is taken from *Manfred* (1.1. 157).

12. See William Empson, *Some Versions of Pastoral* (New York: New Directions, 1974), 208.

13. The tendency to emphasize Byron's penchant for melodrama in this tale over other matters is exemplified in Martin's recent book, *Byron: A Poet before His Public*, 203–4.

14. The extremity of Byron's position here is probably related to his distaste for Wordsworth, which seems to have been particularly strong during these years. In a letter to Hunt in late 1815, for instance, he noted that "there is undoubtedly much natural talent spilt over 'the Excursion' but it is rain upon rocks where it stands & stagnates—or rain upon sands where it falls without fertilizing—who can understand him?—let those who do make him intelligible.—Jacob Behman—Swedenborg—& Joanna Southcote are mere types of this Arch-Apostle of mystery & mysticism" (*BLJ* 4:324). For Byron, nature was not a grand mystery but was subject to specific assessments that, he felt, would undermine (or at least contradict) any idealization of natural process that the mystics could imagine.

15. For a full discussion of Alp's Byronic traits, see Lefevre's essay, "Lord Byron's Fiery Convert of Revenge," *Studies in Philology*, 468–71.

16. For a helpful general discussion of this psychological and social tendency, see G. V. Plekhanov, *Art and Social Life* (1957; reprint ed., Moscow: Progress Publishers, 1977), passim.

17. I am taking this phrase from an unpublished article by Steve Badrich about the historical dimension of *Manfred*.

18. This scene anticipates "Darkness" (written after Byron left England, and within eight months of the publication of *The Siege*), a poem that projects in mythic and universal terms the specific social horrors described here.

Chapter 7. *Parisina*

1. For an excellent discussion of Byron's ambivalent attitude towards his own poetry see McGann, *"Don Juan" in Context*, 1–10.

2. This information is taken from *BCPW* 3:489.

3. Most recent critics seem to prefer *Parisina* to the other narratives, even though the poem has seldom been discussed seriously at any great length. Note, for instance, Leslie A. Marchand's comment that it is "superior in poetic nuances of character and situation to anything in Byron's previous narrative poems" (*Byron's Poetry*, 68).

4. I should note here that McGann goes on to say that "B[yron] used *Parisina* to treat current social and political affairs in a veiled way. B[yron] habitually used older historical situations—and especially people and events from the Italian Renaissance—to highlight

analogous circumstances in the contemporary English and European political scene" (*BCPW* 3:490). While this certainly is true, my own concern is not with history at the conjunctural level, but rather with the deep structure of social relations inscribed in the poem that can be abstracted and discussed in terms of a general social theory. A full analysis of the poem in the terms McGann has in mind remains to be written.

5. For a discussion of the incest theme, see Manning, *Byron and His Fictions*, 58–61.

6. For a discussion of the historical development of the family see Eli Zaretsky, *Capitalism, the Family, & Personal Life* (New York: Harper & Row, 1976), passim.

7. For a discussion of the family in *Werner*, see Watkins, "Byron and the Poetics of Revolution," 95–130.

8. For a discussion of crime in Byron's poetry, again see "Byron and the Poetics of Revolution," 95–130.

9. Anthony Skillen, *Ruling Illusions: Philosophy and Social Order* (Sussex, Eng.: The Harvester Press, 1977), 91.

10. Gramsci, *The Prison Notebooks*, 246.

11. Skillen, *Ruling Illusions*, 91.

12. For a discussion of this idea in other poems by Byron, see Daniel P. Watkins "The Ideological Dimensions of Byron's *The Deformed Transformed*," *Criticism* 25 (1983): 27–39, and "Politics and Religion in Byron's *Heaven and Earth*," *The Byron Journal* 11 (1983): 30–39.

13. Juliet Mitchell, *Psychoanalysis and Feminism* (New York: Vintage Books, 1974), 409.

Chapter 8. Conclusion

1. As McGann says of the general body of Byron's poetry: "Despair is not the meaning of his poetry, it is its condition of being, and the poetic reflex of the social and historical realities it is a part of." For McGann, to see the poems in purely abstract terms as descriptions of the hopeless human condition is to accept uncritically the world-view that they offer, and to overlook the sources of this world-view—to participate, in other words, in "The Romantic Ideology." See *The Romantic Ideology*, 132.

2. Gleckner, *Byron and the Ruins of Paradise*, 99.

3. Note, for instance, Byron's later references to Wordsworth as "Turdsworth" in *BLJ* 7:158, 253, and elsewhere.

4. *The Romantic Ideology*, 145.

5. For a similar discussion of *The Island*, see Paul D. Fleck, "Romance in Byron's *The Island*," in *Byron: A Symposium*, ed. John D. Jump (London and Basingstoke: Macmillan, 1975), 163–83.

6. This is Christopher Hill's phrase used in reference to Milton, but it accurately describes Byron as well. See *Milton and the English Revolution* (New York: The Viking Press, 1977), 5.

7. For a discussion of the dramas along these lines, see Watkins, "Violence, Class Consciousness, and Ideology in Byron's History Plays," 799–816; "The Ideological Dimensions of Byron's *The Deformed Transformed*," 27–39; "Politics and Religion in Byron's *Heaven and Earth*," 30–39; and "Byron and the Poetics of Revolution," 95–130.

8. Again, see Watkins, "Byron and the Poetics of Revolution," 95–130, for a discussion of this subject.

Bibliography

Anderson, Perry. *Passages from Antiquity to Feudalism*. London: New Left Books, 1974.

Belsey, Catherine. *Critical Practice*. London and New York: Methuen, 1980.

Bewley, Marius, ed. *The English Romantic Poets: An Anthology*. New York: The Modern Library, 1970.

Bhaskar, Roy. "On the Possibility of Social Scientific Knowledge and the Limits of Naturalism." In volume 3 of *Issues in Marxist Philosophy*, edited by John Mepham and David-Hillel Ruben. Sussex, Eng.: The Harvester Press, 1979.

Bostetter, Edward E. *The Romantic Ventriloquists: Wordsworth, Coleridge, Keats, Shelley, Byron*. Seattle and London: University of Washington Press, 1963.

Bottomore, Tom, ed. *A Dictionary of Marxist Thought*. Cambridge: Harvard University Press, 1983.

Braudel, Fernand. *On History*. Translated by Sarah Matthews. Chicago and London: The University of Chicago Press, 1980.

Brown, Wallace Cable. "Byron and English Interest in the Near East." *Studies in Philology* 34 (1937): 55–64.

Byron, George Gordon. *Byron's Letters and Journals*. Edited by Leslie A. Marchand. 12 vols. Cambridge: The Belknap Press of Harvard University Press, 1973–82.

———. *Letters and Journals of Lord Byron: With Notices of His Life*. Edited by Thomas Moore. 2 vols. London: 1830.

———. *Lord Byron: The Complete Poetical Works*. Edited by Jerome J. McGann. Vol. 3. Oxford: Oxford University Press, 1981.

———. *The Works of Lord Byron: Letters and Journals*. Edited by Rowland E. Prothero. 6 vols. 1898–1901. Reprint. New York: Octagon Books, Inc., 1966.

———. *The Works of Lord Byron: Poetry*. Edited by Ernest Hartley Coleridge. 7 vols. 1898–1904. Reprint. London and New York: Octagon Books, Inc., 1966.

Calder, Jennie. "The Hero as Lover: Byron and Women." In *Byron: Wrath and Rhyme*, edited by Alan Bold. London: Vision Press Limited; Totowa, N.J.: Barnes & Noble Books, 1983.

Calvert, William J. *Byron: Romantic Paradox*. 1935. Reprint. New York: Russell & Russell, 1962.

Chew, Samuel C. *The Crescent and the Rose: Islam and England during the Renaissance.* 1938. Reprint. New York: Octagon Books, 1965.

———. *The Dramas of Lord Byron.* 1915. Reprint. New York: Russell & Russell, 1964.

Chomsky, Noam. *Language and Responsibility: Based on Conversations with Mitsou Ronat.* Translated by John Viertel. New York: Pantheon Books, 1977.

Coleridge, Samuel T. *Coleridge: Poetical Works.* Edited by Ernest Hartley Coleridge. 1912. Reprint. London and New York: Oxford University Press, 1973.

———. *The Rime of the Ancient Mariner.* Edited by Robert Penn Warren. New York: Reynal and Hitchcock, 1946.

Conant, Martha Pike. *The Oriental Tale in England in the Eighteenth Century.* New York: Columbia University Press, 1908.

Deneau, Daniel P. *Byron's Narrative Poems of 1813: Two Essays.* Salzburg, Austria: Institut für Englische Sprache und Literatur, Universität Salzburg, 1975.

Eagleton, Terry. *Literary Theory: An Introduction.* Minneapolis: University of Minnesota Press, 1983.

Empson, William. *Some Versions of Pastoral.* 1935. Reprint. New York: New Directions, 1974.

Erdman, David V. "Byron and Revolt in England." *Science and Society* 11 (1947): 234–48.

———. "Byron and 'the New Force of the People.'" *Keats-Shelley Journal* 11 (1962): 47–64.

———. "'Fare Thee Well'—Byron's Last Days in England." In *Romantic Rebels: Essays on Shelley and His Circle,* edited by Kenneth Neill Cameron. Cambridge: Harvard University Press, 1973.

———. "Lord Byron." In *Romantic Rebels: Essays on Shelley and His Circle,* edited by Kenneth Neill Cameron. Cambridge: Harvard University Press, 1973.

———. "Lord Byron and the Genteel Reformers." *PMLA* 56 (1941): 1065–94.

———. "Lord Byron as Rinaldo." *PMLA* 57 (1942): 189–231.

Finlay, George. *A History of Greece from its Conquest by the Romans to the Present Time: B.C. 146 to A.D. 1864.* 1877. Reprint. New York: AMS Press, 1970.

Finley, M. I. "Utopianism Ancient and Modern." In *The Critical Spirit: Essays in Honor of Herbert Marcuse,* edited by Kurt H. Wolff and Barrington Moore, Jr. Boston: Beacon Press, 1968.

Fleck, Paul D. "Romance in Byron's *The Island.*" In *Byron: A Symposium,* edited by John D. Jump. London and Basingstoke: Macmillan, 1975.

Gerin, Winifred. "Byron's Influence on the Brontës." *Keats-Shelley Memorial Bulletin* 17 (1966): 1–19.

Gleckner, Robert F. *Byron and the Ruins of Paradise.* Baltimore: The Johns Hopkins University Press, 1967.

Gramsci, Antonio. *Selections from the Prison Notebooks.* Translated and edited by Quintin Hoare and Geoffrey Nowell Smith. New York: International Publishers, 1971.

Habermas, Jurgen. *Communication and the Evolution of Society.* Translated by Thomas McCarthy. Boston: Beacon Press, 1979.

———. *Theory and Practice.* Translated by John Viertel. Boston: Beacon Press, 1973.

Halsted, John, ed. *Romanticism.* New York: Harper & Row, 1969.

Hartman, Geoffrey H. *Wordsworth's Poetry, 1787–1814.* New Haven: Yale University Press, 1964.

Harvey, A. D. *Britain in the Early Nineteenth Century.* New York: St. Martin's Press, 1978.

Hill, Christopher. *Milton and the English Revolution.* New York: The Viking Press, 1977.

———. *The Century of Revolution, 1603–1714.* 1961. Reprint. New York: W. W. Norton, 1966.

Hobsbawm, Edward J. *Bandits.* 1969. Reprint. New York: Pantheon, 1981.

———. *Primitive Rebels: Studies in Archaic Forms of Social Movement in the 19th and 20th Centuries.* New York: W. W. Norton, 1959.

———. *The Age of Revolution: 1789–1848.* New York and Scarborough, Ont.: New American Library, 1962.

Hull, Gloria T. "The Byronic Heroine and Byron's *The Corsair.*" *Ariel* 9 (1978): 71–83.

Jacoby, Russell. *Social Amnesia: A Critique of Conformist Psychology from Adler to Laing.* Boston: Beacon Press, 1975.

Jameson, Fredric. *The Political Unconscious: Narrative as a Socially Symbolic Act.* Ithaca: Cornell University Press, 1981.

Kinnaird, John. *William Hazlitt: Critic of Power.* New York: Columbia University Press, 1978.

Knight, G. Wilson. *Lord Byron: Christian Virtues.* London: Routledge & Kegan Paul, 1952.

Kroeber, Karl. *Romantic Narrative Art.* Madison: The University of Wisconsin Press, 1960.

Lefevre, Carl. "Lord Byron's Fiery Convert of Revenge." *Studies in Philology* 49 (1952): 468–87.

Leontyev, L. *Political Economy: A Condensed Course.* New York: International Publishers, 1974.

Locke, John. *Two Treatises of Government.* Edited by Peter Laslett. Cambridge: Cambridge University Press, 1960.

Lukács, Georg. *Realism in Our Time: Literature and the Class Struggle.* Translated by John and Necke Mander. New York: Harper & Row, 1967.

McGann, Jerome J. *"Don Juan" in Context*. Chicago and London: The University of Chicago Press, 1976.

———. *Fiery Dust: Byron's Poetic Development*. Chicago and London: The University of Chicago Press, 1968.

———. *The Romantic Ideology: A Critical Investigation*. Chicago and London: The University of Chicago Press, 1983.

Macpherson, C. B. *The Political Theory of Possessive Individualism: Hobbes to Locke*. Oxford: The Clarendon Press, 1962.

Manning, Peter J. *Byron and His Fictions*. Detroit: Wayne State University Press, 1978.

———. "Tales and Politics: *The Cosair, Lara,* and *The White Doe of Rylstone*. In *Byron: Poetry and Politics: Seventh International Byron Symposium, Salzburg 1980,* edited by James Hogg. Salzburg, Austria: Institut für Anglistik & Amerikanistik, Universtät Salzburg, 1981.

Marchand, Leslie A. *Byron: A Biography*. 3 vols. New York: Alfred A. Knopf, 1957.

———. *Byron: A Portrait*. New York and London: The University of Chicago Press, 1970.

———. *Byron's Poetry: A Critical Introduction*. Boston: Houghton Mifflin, 1965.

Marshall, William H. "The Accretive Structure of Byron's 'The Giaour.'" *Modern Language Notes* 76 (1961): 502–9.

———. *The Structure of Byron's Major Poems*. Philadelphia: University of Pennsylvania Press, 1962.

Martin, Philip W. *Byron: A Poet before His Public*. Cambridge: Cambridge University Press, 1982.

Marx, Karl. *A Contribution to the Critique of Political Economy*. Translated by S. W. Ryazanskaya. Edited by Maurice Dobb. Moscow: Progress Publishers, 1970.

———. *Capital: A Critique of Political Economy*. Translated by Samuel Moore and Edward Aveling. Edited by Frederick Engels. 1887. Reprint. Moscow: Progress Publishers, 1954.

———. *Economic and Philosophic Manuscripts of 1844*. In *Karl Marx and Frederick Engels: Collected Works*. Vol. 3. New York: International Publishers, 1975.

———. *Grundrisse: Foundations of the Critique of Political Economy*. Translated by Martin Nicolaus. New York: Vintage Books, 1973.

Marx, Karl and Frederick Engels. *The German Ideology*. Moscow: Progress Publishers, 1976.

Melikan, Anahid. *Byron and the East*. Beirut: American University of Beirut, 1977.

Morton, A. L. *A People's History of England*. 1938. Reprint. New York: International Publishers, 1974.

Plekhanov, G. V. *Art and Social Life.* 1957. Reprint. Moscow: Progress Publishers, 1977.

Rapf, Joanna E. "The Byronic Heroine: Incest and the Creative Process." *Studies in English Literature* 21 (1981): 637–45.

Reiman, Donald H., ed. *The Romantics Reviewed: Contemporary Reviews of British Writers. Part B: Byron and Regency Society Poets.* 5 vols. New York and London: Garland Publishing, 1972.

Robinson, Charles E. *Shelley and Byron: The Snake and Eagle Wreathed in Fight.* Baltimore: The Johns Hopkins University Press, 1976.

Rudé, George. *Revolutionary Europe: 1783–1815.* 1964. Reprint. New York: Harper Colophon Books, 1975.

Rousseau, Jean-Jacques. *"On the Social Contract," with "Geneva Manuscript" and "Political Economy."* Translated by Judith R. Masters. Edited by Roger D. Masters. New York: St. Martin's Press, 1978.

Rutherford, Andrew. *Byron: A Critical Study.* Stanford, Calif.: Stanford University Press, 1961.

Said, Edward W. *Orientalism.* 1978. Reprint. New York: Vintage Books, 1979.

Shelley, Percy Bysshe. *The Complete Works of Percy Bysshe Shelley.* Edited by Roger Ingpen and Walter E. Peck. 10 vols. London and New York: The Julian Editions, 1926–30.

Sismondi, John Charles Leonard Simonde de. *A History of the Italian Republics: Being a View of the Rise, Progress, and Fall of Italian Freedom.* New York: Harper & Brothers, 1864.

Skillen, Anthony. *Ruling Illusions: Philosophy and the Social Order.* Sussex, Eng.: The Harvester Press, 1977.

Sweezy, Paul M. *The Present as History: Essays and Reviews on Capitalism and Socialism.* New York: Monthly Review Press, 1953.

Thompson, E. P. *The Making of the English Working Class.* 1963. Reprint. New York: Vintage Books, 1966.

Thorslev, Peter L. *The Byronic Hero: Types and Prototypes.* Minneapolis: University of Minnesota Press, 1962.

Vitale, Marina. "The Domesticated Heroine in Byron's *Corsair* and William Hone's Prose Adaptation." *Literature & History* 10 (1984): 72–94.

Watkins, Daniel P. "Byron and the Poetics of Revolution." *The Keats-Shelley Journal* 34 (1985): 95–130.

———. "The Ideological Dimensions of Byron's *The Deformed Transformed.*" *Criticism* 25 (1983): 27–39.

———. "Politics and Religion in Byron's *Heaven and Earth.*" *The Byron Journal* 11 (1983): 30–39.

———. "Violence, Class Consciousness, and Ideology in Byron's History Plays." *ELH* 48 (1981): 799–816.

Williams, Raymond. *The Country and the City.* London: Chatto and Windus, 1973.

———. *Culture and Society: 1780–1950.* New York: Harper & Row, 1958.

———. *Marxism and Literature.* Oxford: Oxford University Press, 1977.

———. *Problems in Materialism and Culture.* London: New Left Books, 1979.

———. *The Sociology of Culture.* New York: Schocken Books, 1982.

Wilson, Peter B. " 'Galvinism upon Mutton': Byron's Conjuring Trick in *The Giaour.*" *The Keats-Shelley Journal* 24 (1975): 118–27.

Woodring, Carl. *Politics in English Romantic Poetry.* Cambridge: Harvard University Press, 1970.

Wordsworth, William. *The Prelude; or, Growth of a Poet's Mind.* 2d ed. Edited by Ernest de Selincourt, and revised by Helen Darbishire. Oxford: The Clarendon Press, 1959.

Zaretsky, Eli. *Capitalism, the Family, & Personal Life.* New York: Harper & Row, 1976.

Index